D0363825

Idiomantics

Idiomantics

The Weird and Wonderful World of Popular Phrases

Philip Gooden and Peter Lewis

BLOOMSBURY

First published in United Kingdom in 2012 by

Bloomsbury Publishing Plc
50 Bedford Square
London
WC1B 3DP
www.bloomsbury.com

A CIP record for this book is available from the British Library.

ISBN: 9-781-4081-5144-0

This book is produced using paper that is made from wood grown in
managed, sustairable forests. It is natural, renewable and recyclable. The
logging and manufacturing processes conform to the environmental
regulations of the country of origin.

Design by Fiona Pike, Pike Design, Winchester
Typeset by Saxon Graphics Ltd, Derby
Printed in Great Britain by Clays Ltd, St Ives plc

To my mother
Jean Beryl Lewis
1925–2011
who first imbued me with a love of words

CONTENTS

INTRODUCTION

This book is the fruition of our abiding fascination with language. As writers, words are the tools of our trade. But more importantly, words are the tools required for life – for everyone. We think we know what words mean, at least when they are in our own language. Yet, in the case of the idiom, this isn't always so. There are many expressions in both British and American English whose origins are curious or shadowy or contested. And as for idioms from other languages, well, they are a *terra incognita*. Or, as one might say, all Greek to me.

So what is the special lure of idioms? The etymology of the term – via Latin from the Greek adjective *idios*; 'personal' or 'private' – straightaway hints at what's so endlessly interesting about them: their peculiarity. 'Peculiar' both in being particular or unique to the culture whence they come, and in the sense of being downright odd. To cite three random examples – from American English, Dutch and Italian – what on earth are *Swift-boating*, a *monkey sandwich story*, and *Mr Punch's Secret*? All is revealed within.

Idioms tend to lay bare nations' enthusiasms, fixations, antipathies and idiosyncrasies. In keeping with this, we felt free to indulge personal whims when choosing our material for *Idiomantics*. There's no great organising principle at work here, nor do we make any claims to comprehensiveness or complete up-to-dateness. Sure, most phrases in the book are in current usage, but where there was a good yarn to be spun, we haven't let a whiff of obsolescence put us off. This book is less about the destination and more about the fun of getting there (or getting lost, as the case may be).

To nail our colours firmly to the mast: *Idiomantics* is a rag-bag of items beachcombed from the stranger shores of language. Some fascinating information about history, politics, art and literature came to light as we rummaged through our finds. This we now pass on to you, dear reader, with the hope that you'll find it as enthralling as we did. Like guides on some latter-day Grand Tour, we offer it in a spirit of unabashed dilettantism – for all its sometimes negative connotations, it's worth recalling that the root of this word is the Italian verb meaning 'to delight'.

Philip Gooden and Peter Lewis
April 2012

Chapter 1

CURIOUS COVES

The world of idioms is peopled by a large cast of characters, many of them familiar, some less so. Certain phrases in English involve well-known figures from the Bible: 'not to know someone from Adam', 'hard as Pharaoh's heart', 'a Job's comforter'. Even here, though, there's plenty of scope for obscurity. Who remembers who Methuselah was (as in as 'old as Methuselah')? Or knows what's being referred to in the 'law of the Medes and Persians' or 'bow down in the house of Rimmon'?

Beyond Biblical allusions, idiomatic language invokes a whole host of proper names whose origins are now lost forever. We trot out phrases like 'the life of Riley', 'the real McCoy' and 'all my eye and Betty Martin' with no idea who these individuals were, or if they even existed.

This chapter explores some of the factual and fictional characters who have lent their names to everyday phrases. Unashamedly, though, we have chosen to major here on foreign usages, some of which have a surprising provenance…

LAUGH LIKE BOLLE ON THE MILK FLOAT (GERMAN)

Sich wie die Bolles uffn Milchwagen amüsieren – **to laugh like a drain/be as happy as Larry**

Berlin grew like Topsy in the 19th century. Its population of just over 170,000 in 1800 had mushroomed to 826,000 by 1871, the year the Second German Empire was founded. And it kept on climbing steeply: it had risen to two million around the turn of the century and four million by the start of the First World War. A vastly increased supply of goods and services was needed to keep pace with this massive expansion and the period witnessed the rise of some dynamic entrepreneurs. Carl Julius Andreas Bolle (1832–1910) was one such: starting out as a humble bricklayer's apprentice, by the 1860s he had moved on to selling ice for keeping perishable goods fresh, chipped from the winter floes on Berlin's rivers. He then diversified into selling sea fish, growing fruit and making preserves. But his most successful venture by far was the dairy he founded in 1881. By the following year, he had a fleet of 56 horse-drawn carts delivering fresh milk to the metropolis. These floats, with their characteristic bell to attract customers, were a familiar sight on the city's streets for decades.

Bolle is a common Berlin surname, and some time before the advent of Carl's dairy business, a popular song in the local dialect about a typically rumbustious, happy-go-lucky Berliner of this name had been doing the rounds. Its refrain ran: *Aber dennoch hat sich Bolle janz köstlich amüsiert* ('But Bolle just laughed it all off'). In time – and a testament to how ubiquitous Carl Bolle's product had become – this catchphrase was embellished with *uffn Milchwagen* ('on the milk float'). Nobody quite knows why: it could simply be that milkmen soon gained a reputation as cheery, chirpy fellows. But one commentator has suggested that Bolle's employees got a kick out of driving their carts fast through puddles, drenching passers-by. This would lend their amusement that quintessentially German edge of *Schadenfreude*.

THE REAL McCOY (US)

The real thing, the genuine article

There are various explanations as to who or what the original McCoy (or MacKay) was. The most plausible ultimate derivation is from the Scottish distillers Mackay & Co who, if not the creators of the phrase 'the real Mackay', certainly used it in their advertising from the 1870s. Within a few years, and after crossing the Atlantic, the Mackay part of the expression mutated into the Irish form of McCoy. Once in the US, it attached itself to at least three figures. One was a cattle baron, Joseph McCoy, who was shipping up to half a million head of cattle every year from Kansas to Chicago during the 1870s. Another was Elijah McCoy, the Canadian-born son of fugitive slaves who invented a lubricating cup for oiling a locomotive while it was in motion and so eliminated the need for frequent stops. A third was the boxer 'Kid' McCoy (real name Norman Selby), who supposedly had to face down imitators and who, when he won a match in San Francisco, was headlined as the 'real McCoy'.

Since the expression is designed to distinguish the fake or the inferior from the genuine article, the association with the boxer is the one most likely responsible for the continued currency of the 'real McCoy'. The cattle baron was not competing against anyone using the same name, and although there have been some attempts to link Elijah to the phrase – on the grounds that railway engineers looking for the best lubricant would ask for the 'real McCoy' – these seem to belong more to a revisionary version of African-American historical achievement than to any usage which emerged at the time. It is ironically apt, however, that there should be several competing claimants to the title of the 'real McCoy'.

KNOW MORE THAN LEPE (Spanish)

Saber más (or Más listo) que Lepe – **to be very smart/a fount of knowledge/a walking encyclopedia**

Nowadays, our models of egg-headedness are scientists or

witty cultural commentators – think Stephen Hawking or Stephen Fry. A sign of these secular times; but in 18th-century Spain, when this phrase was coined, the epitome of a person with a brain the size of a planet was a man of the cloth. Pedro de Lepe y Dorantes was born in 1641 at Sanlúcar de Barrameda in the Cádiz region of Andalucia, taught humanities at the universities of Seville and Salamanca, was ordained a priest in 1667 and appointed Bishop of Calahorra and la Calzada (in the Rioja region) in 1686, a post he remained in until his death in 1700.

Lepe earned his reputation for sagacity from his authorship of the catchily titled *Catecismo católico, en el cual se contiene la explicación de los principales misterios de nuestra santa católica fe y las demás cosas que debe el cristiano saber para su salvación* ('Catholic Catechism, in which is contained an explanation of all the principal mysteries of our Sacred Catholic faith and of other matters that any Christian needs to know for his salvation'). This handbook of religious observance became a bestseller among the God-fearing people of Spain in the 17th and 18th centuries, providing comprehensive answers to all questions regarding the Seven Sacraments (Baptism, Confirmation, Holy Communion, Confession, Marriage, Holy Orders and the Anointing of the Sick).

As uncritical reverence for the Church declined, so the idiom was tweaked for comic effect: later variants include *saber más que Lepe, su hija y su hijo* ('to know more than Lepe, his daughter and his son' – a scurrilous, but by no means implausible, suggestion in the case of a Catholic priest) and the neatly rhyming *saber más que Lepe, Lepijo y el que lo dijo* ('to know more than Lepe, Lepijo [a diminutive form] and the person who coined the phrase').

The Spanish historian Pedro Voltes (1926–2009) claims that the idiom derives not from Pedro de Lepe but Juan de Lepe, an earlier Spanish adventurer. According to Voltes' 1994 book *El reverso de la historia* (vol. 4), after roaming far and wide, Lepe fetched up in England in the late 1400s, where he became friends with King Henry VII. When they were engaged on one occasion in their favourite pastime of playing cards, the king staked control over his realm for one day on a hand, and lost. From his 24-hour reign over Tudor England, the Spaniard reputedly acquired enough wealth to return to his native country and live in comfort for the rest of his life.

FURPHY (Australian)

A rumour

John Furphy was a manufacturer of farm equipment in the state of Victoria at the close of the 19th century. His most notable product was an item which he never patented, a water cart consisting of a 180-gallon iron cylinder on a horse-drawn wooden frame. The name of the manufacturer was painted in large capitals on each side of the tank and, Furphy being a devout man, moralising slogans were inscribed on the rear of the cylinder. The carts were created for transporting water on farms and were used in large numbers by the Australian army in the First World War. Once towed into camp, the water carts were usually parked close to the latrines, the one area where the men were able to gossip and exchange stories away from the watchful eye of the officers. In addition, the drivers of the 'furphies' were themselves notorious for spreading rumours from place to place. In this way, the name of the manufacturer/truck swiftly became a slang term for a rumour or even a lie.

Current use equates a furphy with a falsehood ('Being both fat and fit may not be a furphy'[1]; 'Furphies a'plenty in long ANZUS alliance'[2]). This expression, which has never travelled outside Australia, is the equivalent of the US 'scuttlebutt'.

There are a couple of curious sanitary equivalents to 'furphy', also drawn from service slang even if not in current use. One is 'Elsan gen', referring to information which can't be relied on and deriving from the trade name of the portable lavatories that use chemicals to neutralise the waste. Elsans – the word is an amalgamation of the first two initials of the inventor Ephraim Louis Jackson and 'sanitation' – were installed on bombers at the same time as 'gen' emerged as RAF slang for 'information'. The other word from the Second World War is 'latrinogram', a technically advanced version of the 'latrine rumour' which first saw the light of day in 1918. (see also **Scuttlebutt**)

GET YOURSELF FRANZED (GERMAN)

Sich verfranzen – **to get hopelessly lost**

This verb is still in current German usage, but derives from a long-since obsolete bit of pilots' argot. During the First World War, when everything about flying was still very much on a wing and a prayer, navigation was rudimentary in the extreme. In two-seater aircraft – the very first military machines, used initially for battlefield spotting, plus the occasional crude bomb drop, by hand – this involved the observer consulting a map, a watch and a compass in order to work out the plane's speed and

1 'Being both fat and fit may not be a furphy' *Sydney Morning Herald*, 25 March 2010.
2 'Furphies a'plenty in long ANZUS alliance' *Canberra Times*, 18 November 2011.

course and so determine its position. The generic term for a navigator/observer in the Imperial German flying corps was 'Franz', while that for a pilot was 'Emil' (a practice echoed in RAF slang for a bomber's rear gunner in the Second World War – 'tail-end Charlie'). From this there arose the verb *franzen* (now defunct), meaning 'to navigate by dead reckoning'. By extension, to go astray was conveyed by the reflexive *sich verfranzen*; in German the prefix *ver*- frequently negates a verb, as in *lernen* (to learn) and *verlernen* (to forget something you've learnt).

But why 'Franz' and 'Emil'? This may have something to do with standard voice procedure in radio communication. The German equivalent of 'Echo', which in the NATO spelling alphabet represents the letter E in an aircraft's call sign, is 'Emil'. And although F is now 'Friedrich' and not 'Franz', it may well be that the latter was the original designation. The alphabet has certainly changed several times. The Nazis, for example, were so thoroughgoing in their racism that they expunged all Jewish-sounding names such as David, Nathan, Samuel and Zacharias from the alphabet, replacing them with Dora, Nordpol, Siegfried and Zeppelin. Most, though not all, of the former names have since been reinstated.

THE FULL MONTY (UK)
Everything, the lot

Just as the Americans have their 'whole nine yards', the British have 'the full Monty', two expressions which are identical in meaning ('the works', 'the whole lot') and equally obscure in origin. Of the two, 'the full Monty' is the more recent, with the earliest dictionary citation being dated to 1985 although the term appears to have provided the name of a Manchester chip shop before that according to the *Oxford English Dictionary*.[3] The expression is sometimes laid at the door of Field Marshal Montgomery, victor of the battle of El Alamein and famously nicknamed 'Monty'. Suggestions that the 'full' relates to his long-winded briefings or the large number of medals he wore seem more the product of desperation than common sense, while the connection with the full English breakfasts which Monty apparently enjoyed each morning during the North African campaign ignore the relatively recent emergence of the phrase 'full English' to describe breakfast (like the ploughman's lunch, the meal is not really a tradition at all). No, the Field Marshal can be safely dismissed.

The 'full Monty' is often connected to the chain of tailors founded by Montague Burton. Customers in search of a three-piece suit would supposedly ask for 'the full Monty'. The northern links for the earliest citations of the term together with the Yorkshire roots of the company make this at least a possible origin. The expression was really given a boost by the eponymous 1997 film which featured a group of unemployed Sheffield steel workers who regain some control over their lives by forming a Chippendales-style group, stripping down before crowds of local lasses and going the 'full Monty'. (see also **the whole nine yards**)

---

3 'Earlier currency is app. implied by the following names of fish and chip shops: 1982 Yellow pages: Manchester North 264/3 Fully Monty Chippy The, 30 Townley St, Middleton; Fullmonty Chippy, 61 Radclyffe St, Chadderton. Oxford English Dictionary. Oxford: Oxford University Press.

MY NAME IS HARE, I KNOW NOTHING
(GERMAN)

Mein Name ist Hase, ich weiß von nichts – **nothing to do with me, mate**

In 1854, a member of one of the student fraternities at the University of Heidelberg killed his opposite number in a duel. Now, as Jerome K. Jerome pointed out in *Three Men on the Bummel* (1900), the whole idea of these militaristic clubs and their staged combats was to scar the face of your opponent permanently (a mutilation he'd wear with pride for ever after), not murder him, so the perpetrator immediately took to his heels. Whether through theft or complicity, to cover his tracks while on the run our villain used the identity papers of his fellow student Karl Victor von Hase (1834–60), son of an eminent Protestant church historian and theologian from Jena, Karl August von Hase. (*Hase* is the German word for 'hare'.)

The miscreant was eventually caught and put on trial in Strasbourg, to where Karl Victor was also summoned to account for himself. When he appeared before the court, charged with assisting a fugitive, he is reputed to have made the following brief statement: *Mein Name ist Hase. Ich verneine alle Gegenfragen. Ich weiß von nichts.* ('My name is Hase. I refuse to be cross-examined. I know nothing about this.')

It isn't recorded whether Hase was sent down, but the court of public opinion instantly found him guilty, taking up his laconic defence and putting it to ironic use as an implausible protestation of dumb innocence. And so it has remained to the present day.

MURPHY'S LAW (US?)

A proverbial 'law' which contends that 'if anything can go wrong, it will'

There is no agreement over the source for this well-known law of human life and endeavour, not even a consensus as to whether there was ever a Murphy to give his name to the law in the first place. Yet one well-documented account does have a Captain Edward Murphy christening the law in the late 1940s during US Air Force tests on the gravitational effects on pilots of rapid deceleration. When gauges measuring the experiments were found to have been wired the wrong way round by his assistant, resulting in a zero reading, Murphy is supposed to have made an observation along the lines that if one way of doing a job will end in disaster then someone, sooner or later, will do it that way. On the other hand, and according to John Glenn – one of the earliest astronauts and the first American to orbit the earth – Murphy never existed. Rather, he was 'a fictitious character who appeared in a series of educational cartoons put out by the US Navy [...] a careless, all-thumbs mechanic who was prone to make such mistakes as installing a propeller backwards.' If this is so, Murphy's law would seem to be more 'don't do as I do', a warning to be vigilant, rather than a wry comment on human activity.

Whoever Murphy was, or whether he even existed, the idea that his law embodies – that where things can go wrong, they will – is surely as old as humanity itself. The essence of its operation is perfectly encapsulated in a story told by author Rob Eastaway, who was invited to talk on radio about just this subject: 'I took a slice of toast into the *Today* programme studio to demonstrate that when you slide a piece of toast off a table, the laws of nature actually determine that it will do a half twist and land butter-side-down, so Murphy's law is destined to happen. Unfortunately, the piece of toast I used had curled up at the corners so when I shoved it, it glided instead of twisting and landed on the floor butter-side-up. Thinking on my feet, I explained that my experiment to demonstrate Murphy's law had gone wrong, which was great as it had therefore been a perfect demonstration of Murphy's law in action.'

Sod's law, often cited as being the same as Murphy's, belongs to British rather than American English and, surprisingly, seems to have been coined quite recently (first seen in print in *New Statesman*, 1970). It is sometimes claimed that Sod's law applies to accidents of fate or fortune, often quite minor ones, like rainy bank holidays or the doorbell ringing as you get in the shower. By contrast, Murphy's law applies more to human miscalculation, incompetence and fallibility.

BEHAVE LIKE EARL BOWLER OF THE GASWORKS (GERMAN)

Sich wie Graf Koks von der Gasanstalt benehmen – **to give yourself airs and graces**

This idiom dates from the late 19th century and is used predominantly in the larger conurbations of north Germany, especially the industrial Ruhr region and Berlin. It's a fascinating example of an idiomatic *faux ami*, hinting at a simple derivation but ultimately turning out to be far more complex and interesting.

The principal meaning of the German masculine noun *Koks* is 'coke' – the main by-product of the manufacture of town gas from coal. At first sight, then, we seem to be dealing with some mythical figure called 'Count (or Earl) Coke' (perhaps a relative of the English 'Lord Muck'?), the irony of his noble title heightened by the bathetic inclusion of his demesne as 'the gasworks'.

But this plausible explanation turns out to be as evanescent as coal gas. *Koks* also happens to be a colloquial term for a bowler hat (the standard word is *die Melone*, from its shape). Why *Koks*? While the English chose to immortalise the hat's maker, the Germans commemorate the man who commissioned it – the 2nd Earl of Leicester, Thomas William *Coke* (1822–1909). The sire of Holkham Hall in Norfolk, Coke had the bowler made as a sturdy and practical riding hat for his head gamekeeper and staff. As contemporary sketches show, the Earl was so pleased with the finished article that he even took to wearing it himself.

Before long, bowlers were all the rage, not just in London and England at large, but on the Continent as well. The gentlemanly associations of this fine English headgear gave it a certain cachet among those who fancied themselves as a cut above. Young *flâneurs* about town sport them in the German Expressionist painter Ernst Ludwig Kirchner's scenes of louche Berlin nightlife in the 1910s. Another group who favoured the bowler were bailiffs employed by the gas company to dun customers for unpaid bills. Here, then, is the true source of the idiom.

Despite the best efforts of generations of marauding football fans, the idea of the English gentleman still holds continental Europe spellbound. John Steed from *The Avengers* remains an evergreen favourite – the programme's German title is *Mit Schirm, Charme und Melone* ('With a brolly, charm and a bowler hat').

UNCLE SAM (US)

The personification of the United States government; the American people

The figure that comes to personify a nation, whether by accident or design, will reflect some aspect of that country.

The archetypal Englishman John Bull – traditional, stubborn, a bit dense and fond of his roast beef (*les rosbifs* is the mild insult the French still direct at the English) – began as a semi-satirical creation in the early 1700s but was regarded more with respect than amusement thereafter. The feminine figure of Marianne represents France but her embodiment of the abstract virtues such as liberty and reason which underlie the Republic may be obscured by the fact that since 1969, real women have been used as models for the image on coins and notes, town-hall busts and so on. Brigitte Bardot was the first real-life Marianne.

Uncle Sam sometimes stands for the American people but, more frequently, he is the face of their government. He is at least 200 years old. There is a story that the name was acquired from one Samuel Wilson, who supplied meat to the army during the 1812 war against the British. The 'US' initials, standing for United States, which were stamped on the barrels of meat were conflated with a jokey reference to the 'Uncle Sam' who was feeding the troops. There does not appear to be any strong evidence in favour of this, however, and it is more likely that the name was created in reverse, as it were, by taking the abbreviated form of the country and then attaching to those initials a half-humorous but imaginary persona. During the Civil War, the image of Uncle Sam grew a beard and became associated with that of Abraham Lincoln while in both World Wars he appeared on recruiting posters with pointing forefinger and the Kitchener-like demand: 'I WANT YOU FOR [the] US ARMY.'

The identification of the state and its government with an uncle figure is not entirely coincidental. If the land where one is born is the mother country (fatherland has unfortunate overtones), the authorities who run it are more like uncles. And although uncles ought to be benign – or avuncular – there is nothing to say that they will not turn out to be as murderous as Claudius, the uncle of Hamlet. It is worth remembering that 'uncle' was once English slang for a pawnbroker, someone you might be forced to turn to in time of crisis – but not without paying a price for it.

BOB'S YOUR UNCLE! (UK)
There you are!/Job done!

There is one straightforward but probably erroneous explanation for this peculiarly English phrase. Arthur Balfour was born into the Victorian aristocracy and elected to parliament in his mid-twenties. In 1887 he was appointed as Chief Secretary to Ireland by his uncle Robert Cecil, the Marquess of Salisbury, and three-time premier. Fifteen years later when Cecil stepped down from his final stint in office, the post passed to his nephew, who then served as prime minister from 1902–1905. Either of these promotions for Balfour is supposed to have prompted the phrase 'Bob's your uncle!' because of his link with Robert Cecil. But the phrase, rather than being a cynical comment on the power of nepotism, simply describes a feat which is easily and satisfactorily accomplished. The Balfour explanation may, therefore, be a little too neat. If it was coined after Balfour was given the Irish post, then almost half a century elapsed before the expression first appeared in print – an unusually long period for a phrase to exist only in spoken form. The *Oxford English Dictionary* cites the poet Stephen Spender referring (in 1946) to the expression as a 'Cockney phrase'. This seems a world away from a parliamentary witticism.

There was a music hall song recorded by Florrie Ford in 1931 and called 'Follow Your Uncle Bob'. The uncle in question, though he's getting on, seems to be a bit of a lad since he is referred to as 'naughty but nice' and a 'son of a gun'. More to the point, the song includes the refrain 'Bob's your uncle'. It is possible that the expression derived from the song but just as likely, indeed more likely, is that the song was created out of a popular catchphrase whose precise origins remain obscure.

POTEMKIN VILLAGES (GERMAN)
Potemkinsche Dörfer – **Castles in the air**

The German idiom, which by now has also become a familiar usage in English, derives from the fake villages supposedly erected in the Crimea by Russian Count Grigori Alexandrovich Potemkin. A favourite of Catherine the Great, Field Marshal Potemkin (1739–91) won fame during the Russo-Turkish Wars of the 1770s and 1780s, which brought the Crimea and the whole northern coast of the Black Sea under Russian control. When the Empress visited her newly won territories in 1787, Potemkin is said to have constructed sham settlements along the Dnieper River, complete with freshly painted woodwork, flowers and smiling 'inhabitants,' to impress upon his mistress how far pacification and civilisation of the region had progressed. These empty façades were cleared away once the imperial entourage had passed. Although most modern commentators now dismiss the story as propaganda used against Potemkin by his many enemies, the idiom stuck. Indeed, the attributive noun 'Potemkin' can now be used to denote anything illusory, deceptive or just plain ineffectual.

Benito Mussolini once proclaimed: 'The Liberal State is a mask behind which there is no face; it is a scaffolding behind which there is no building', but ironically he was himself a past master in the art of empty window-dressing. The visit to Rome by his Axis partner Adolf Hitler on 3–9 May 1938 provided him with the ideal opportunity to indulge his over developed sense of the theatrical. The German chancellor's train arrived at night at the specially constructed Ostiense railway station south of the city centre. On the three-mile route taken by the motorcade to the royal palace on the Quirinal Hill, Hitler, in the company of Mussolini and King Victor Emmanuel II, was driven past a series of elaborate stage sets, intended to highlight and enhance famous landmarks of the Eternal City. Constructed by a prominent designer from the Rome Opera House, these involved huge columns topped by gas-lit candelabra receding in long colonnades towards dramatically floodlit focal points like the Arch of Constantine and the Colosseum. The columns were decked out with the Italian *fasces* and the German swastika. The symbolism was unmistakable: Mussolini's fascist state was the natural heir to the Roman *Imperium*. A grand piece of Potemkinesque bombast from the 'strutting, sawdust Roman Caesar' (William L. Shirer).

NASCAR DAD (US)

Generally a working-class male figure regarded by politicians as an important vote

NASCAR is the acronym of the National Association for Stock Car Auto Racing. This colourful and sometimes destructive motor sport is thought to appeal in particular to white and middle-aged working men. This represents a very significant demographic in US politics, one capable by itself of swinging election results. 'Nascar dad' was first identified in 2002 as a target group for recruiting by Democrats, who had lost much of the working-class vote to the Republicans. The concept was prominent in the 2004 presidential election, which the Democrats nevertheless lost. In the United Kingdom, there had been an earlier attempt to link cars with a male figure who was both working-class and a potential swing voter in the alliterative concept of 'Mondeo man'. Like Nascar Dad, the British version was supposedly one of the keys to electoral victory. A feebly alliterative counterpart to Mondeo man is the market researchers' representative female, known as 'Worcester woman'.

Car-driving is also the source of the US female near-equivalent to Nascar man, in the shape of either 'soccer mom' or 'hockey mom'. In this case the woman's role is to drive her children to the school soccer or hockey matches and no doubt to stay and cheer on the sidelines. Sarah Palin famously described herself as a hockey mom when she was campaigning for the Vice-Presidency in 2008. Although the expression might be seen as reductive by emphasising the mother's traditional role in running the household, it appeals to a traditional and conservative segment of the US electorate. In the same way, the variant phrase 'security mom', coined after the 9/11 attacks, underlined the value to politicians of playing the national-defence card when appealing to women voters. (see also **John Q. Public**)

MR PUNCH'S SECRET (ITALIAN)
Un segreto di Pulcinella – **an open secret**

Before evolving into the wife-beating, child-abusing favourite of British seaside entertainment, Mr Punch was the Italian *commedia dell'arte* character Pulcinella.

Mr Punch's delinquency follows a set routine; like all comic figures down the ages, he has a *shtick*. Likewise, the stock characters of the *commedia dell'arte* genre were stereotypes playing prescribed roles: Pantalone was the rich, miserly cuckold; Arlecchino (Harlequin) the cheeky but loyal servant; Scaramuccia (Scaramouche) the boastful buffoon, and so on.

For his part, Pulcinella was a rumbustious trickster from Naples – a place, then as now, notorious for having more than its fair share of dodgy characters surviving on their wits. A devil-may-care vulgarity and garrulousness are central to his nature, and one of the chief ways these traits manifest themselves is through his shameless indiscretion. In no time, a confidence shared with Pulcinella is all round the town.

Pulcinella is both incorrigible and unrepentant; English has enshrined his self-satisfied roguishness and recidivism in the idiom 'as pleased as Punch', which dates from around the late 18th century.

HOBSON'S CHOICE (UK)

Used to describe a situation in which there is in fact no choice, with only one path or option available to be taken

The old expression 'Hobson's choice' is occasionally used as if it described a dilemma[4], a choice between unpalatable alternatives. In fact, the expression characterises a situation in

---

4 A dilemma may also be referred to as 'Morton's fork', named after an Archbishop of Canterbury during the reign of Henry VII. A method of enforcing loans to the crown, Morton's fork worked on the principle that those rich men who displayed their wealth could afford to pay while the ones who lived without ostentation must have money put aside and, therefore, could also afford to pay. The victim was impaled on one of the two prongs of the pitchfork but the result was the same. Morton was an early proponent of **Catch-22** (see p.89).

which, even if you might have been expecting to choose, you can take only what is on offer and nothing else. It derives from Thomas Hobson, who hired out horses in Cambridge in the 16th century. He observed that Cambridge was a place where 'the scholars rid hard' and that if customers were left to pick for themselves they inevitably selected the best and fastest horses, which soon lost those qualities as a result. Hobson's solution was to compel every visitor either to hire the horse which was nearest to the stable-door or to leave empty-handed. His reasoning was that 'every customer was alike well-served according to his chance, and every horse ridden with the same justice.' Hobson must have conducted his life with the same degree of organisation as he ran his business for he died in 1631 at what was then the considerable age of 87.

HAVE THE BRISK OTTO (GERMAN)
Den flotten Otto haben – **to have the runs**

For all their many admirable and endearing qualities, Germans have an unhealthy interest in bowel movements. Or perhaps that should be 'healthy', since it's born of a hypochondriac concern with wellbeing so ingrained it's little short of a national obsession. In her 1973 novel *Fear of Flying,* Erica Jong got to the seat of the matter with her thumbnail sketch of toilets around the world. The German WC is, she wrote: '…a fixture unlike any other in the world. It has a cute little porcelain platform for the shit to fall on so you can inspect it before it whirls off into the watery abyss…'

'Otto' is an old German forename, redolent of Prussians with stiff collars and extravagant sideburns. Latterly, it's started coming back into vogue among middle-class parents (like the Harry/Henry/George resurgence in England), but for a long time it languished in the lumber-room of archaic and faintly ludicrous names to foist on a child. And in north German dialect, 'ein Otto' means 'a whopper'. History's most famous Otto was, of course, Bismarck, the colossus of European politics in the mid- to late 19th century. He apparently had an appetite to match, downing heroic quantities of *foie gras* and champagne. We're just a whisker away from pulling all this information together and tracing our phrase back to some scabrous contemporary swipe at the *Reichskanzler*'s epicurean and excretory excesses. But alas, it's not to be; despite his time bomb of a diet, there's nothing to link Bismarck and diarrhoea.

So, in all likelihood, it all just comes down to the 'big 'un' meaning of 'Otto' teamed with the pleasing alliteration of the adjective 'flott' (brisk, quick, speedy, zippy).

JOHN Q. PUBLIC (US)
The average citizen

This is one of several terms used to characterise the average American citizen, a counterpart to the British John Smith or Fred/Joe Bloggs. The character of John Q. Public was the invention of a 20-year old newspaper cartoonist called Vaughn Shoemaker, who began his career on the *Chicago Daily News* and who went on to win two Pulitzer Prizes for his later work. Shoemaker's 1922 creation of John Q. Public stood for the typical, hard-pressed American taxpayer. The name caught on and was soon being used across the United States. Variants include John Q., John Q. Citizen and Jane Q. Public. The use of a middle initial is distinctively American. It is possible that the Q. is a reminder of John Quincy Adams, sixth president of the US and son of one of the Founding Fathers.

Much older than John Q. Public is the name John Doe, which was invented for legal purposes to do with landowning and originated in England in medieval times. The title is still used in the US to represent an anonymous party in a law suit or an unidentified corpse or hospital patient. Jane Doe and Baby Doe are also found in these contexts. Where John is the relatively formal way of referring to the typical citizen, Joe is the casual version, as in Joe Citizen, working Joe, GI Joe (and GI Jane). Specialised variations include the Yiddish form of Joe Schmo; Joe Six-pack, so called for his preference for beer rather than his stomach muscles; and Joe Blow, possibly named after the supporting player in a wind band. During the 2008 presidential campaign, a real-life individual was christened by the media as 'Joe the plumber', despite the fact that his first name was actually Samuel and that he was not an accredited plumber. Nevertheless, he came to stand for the average working American and was frequently mentioned by candidates John McCain and Barack Obama.

GÖTZ VON BERLICHINGEN! (German: name of the eponymous character in a 1773 play by Goethe)
[circumlocution for] You can kiss my arse!

Part of the agenda of the *Sturm und Drang* ('Storm and Stress') movement in German literature in the 1770s, of which the young Johann Wolfgang von Goethe was a member, was to make a clean break with the theatre of the past. In the case of Goethe's first play *Götz von Berlichingen*, written when he was 24 years old, this not only meant dispensing with the Aristotelian unities of time and place that had governed dramatic action but also having characters speak in an earthy vernacular far removed from the genteel milieu of the French classical models that had up till then held sway on the German stage.

Thus it is that the hero of Goethe's drama, who is loosely based on the historical figure of an infamous 16th-century Swabian mercenary, gives this uncompromising response when called upon to surrender his castle to a besieging army: 'Tell your captain that I have, as ever, due respect for His Imperial Majesty, but that as far as he himself is concerned, he can lick me in the arse!' So notorious did these lines become that, over time, the title of the play came to be used as a euphemism for the phrase *leck mich am Arsch*.

SOME OTHER JOHNS

'John' may no longer be the most frequently used given first name in the English-speaking world, but as itself or in variant forms like 'Jack' and 'Joe' it forms the basis for hundreds of expressions, from the respectable to the scurrilous, including:

John Hancock The term is used in the United States for someone's signature (as in 'Just put your John Hancock here'), because Hancock was the first signatory to the Declaration of Independence and because his signature was particularly large and decisive.

John Thomas The penis. In the middle of the 19th century, the name was a colloquial reference to a servant in livery. The association between man and member may be, as slang dictionaries speculate, because the servant is expected to stand up in the presence of a lady. An early version of D. H. Lawrence's once notorious novel *Lady Chatterley's Lover* was entitled *John Thomas and Lady Jane*.

Dear John The opening of a letter from the wife/ sweetheart of someone in the US armed forces, explaining that she plans to leave him, usually because she has found someone else. According to one American newspaper, the expression as well as the experience were common enough by the end of the Second World War for the men to refer to them simply as 'Dear Johns' or a 'dearjohn'.

Cousin John In the shortened form of 'cuz john', this was US slang for lavatory ('john' is still used in this sense). The fact that it was slang at Harvard in the 18th century suggests that it was a humorous reference. One can imagine someone slipping out of a room, announcing that he was off to see cousin John. Later British versions are 'spending a penny' and 'seeing a man about a dog/horse'. As a kind of anti-euphemism, Barry Humphries coined the more direct 'point percy at the porcelain', among many other Australianisms.

Chapter 2

PURSUITS AND PASTIMES

At root, idioms testify to the human urge to play; they are the trick shots, the showy set pieces of speech which, as a foreign-language learner, you can't wait to use to try and impress your interlocutors with your skill. But, as in sports, if you fail to pull them off successfully, you fall flat on your face.

The German philosopher and playwright Friedrich Schiller maintained that people only become sublimely human when they're at play. On our most basic level of existence, we plod along with feet of clay as *Homo sapiens*, but it's as *Homo ludens* that we really spread our wings.

So, let the games begin!

THROW ONE'S HAT INTO THE RING (UK/US)
To announce one's candidacy for (political) office

Come the 19th century, hats had replaced gloves as way of offering a fight. Just as the medieval knight threw down his gauntlet for his opponent to pick up if the challenge were accepted, the onlooker at a boxing competition in the early 1800s would throw his hat into the ring to signify a willingness to take part. As a method of capturing attention, the hat-throwing would likely have been more effective than shouting at an already noisy venue and the bareheaded man would stand out at a time when almost everyone wore some sort of head covering. It seems to have taken the best part of a century for the expression to acquire its metaphorical sense. When Theodore Roosevelt was asked about being a candidate for the Republican presidential nomination in 1912, he declared in best macho style: 'My hat is in the ring. The fight is on and I am stripped to the buff'. The hat-in-the-ring was made literal again during the First World War when, in the shape of a stars-and-stripes top hat inside a hoop, it was used as the insignia for one of the first US air squadrons to be committed to the Western Front.

Since then, the expression has never looked back. Whenever anyone puts themselves up for a post, they are said to be throwing their hat into the ring. One of the marks of a useful metaphor is its adaptability. In 1940, the 38-year-old Thomas E. Dewey announced he was standing for the US presidency and was mocked by an opponent because he had 'tossed his diapers [nappies] into the ring'. Throwing 'her curls in the ring' was the headline when the one-time child film star Shirley Temple announced her candidacy for Congress in 1967. And, more recently, when the governor of the US state of New Mexico toyed with the idea of running for president, what else would he toss into the ring (according to the press) but his sombrero? Metaphors can get out of control, though. As a Tea Party (right-wing) presidential wannabe flirted with the idea of candidacy in 2011, the *Vanity Fair* blog commented: 'Michele Bachmann to Throw Her Teabag-Covered Tricorn Hat in Presidential Ring.'[1]

(Boxing also provides another 'throw' metaphor in 'throw in the towel', the action of a second or trainer when he threw a towel into the ring as a signal that his man was conceding defeat. An earlier equivalent is 'throwing up the sponge'.)

---

1 'Michele Bachmann to Throw Her Teabag-Covered Tricorn Hat in Presidential Ring.' Julie Weiner, *Vanity Fair* Blog, 24 March, 2011: www.vanityfair.com/online/daily/2011/03/michele-bachmann-to-throw-her-teabag-covered-tricorne-hat-in-presidential-ring

HIT THE GROUND RUNNING (US)

To start on a new project or task with energy and speed

With its macho and military overtones, this is a popular idiom on both sides of the Atlantic when there is a change of government. The newcomers want to present themselves as a no-nonsense, can-do bunch of professionals (unlike the previous lot) who will waste no time fulfilling all those promises they made while out on the campaign trail. The metaphorical practice of 'hitting the ground running' also finds a natural home in sport and any other activity requiring vigour and pace. At first glance, it seems the expression must originate with the military and be dated no earlier than the Second World War, since it evokes the image of a sea- or airborne soldier going into action the moment his feet touch the ground. But there is some evidence of the phrase being in use before this, even if its precise origins are disputed. One possible source is the triple action of the highly skilled (American) football player who is able to jump, catch the ball and then hit the ground running (of course, any good rugby player should be able to do this). Less likely is that it described the way a hobo or vagrant would leap from a freight train as it was slowing down. The most colourful explanation goes right back to the days of the pony express to describe the moment when riders arriving at the change station would leap from one mount and run to the next. There is a US Navy variant of 'hitting the deck running', a formula employed by captains in their reports on new junior officers and not meaning much more than that the newcomer has checked aboard.

NOT LEAVE A SINGLE PUPPET WITH ITS HEAD ON (Spanish)

No dejar/quedar títere con cabeza – **to take no prisoners/ to trash the joint**

In Part II, Chapter 26 of Miguel de Cervantes' epic picaresque novel *Don Quixote* (1605), the eponymous hero and his sidekick Sancho Panza are treated to a puppet show in the courtyard of an inn, staged by one Maese Pedro ('Master Peter'). The drama that the papier-mâché marionettes perform is *The Tale of Melisendra*, a story about the adoptive daughter of Charlemagne, who before the action unfolds has been abducted by the Moors and taken to Zaragoza, where she is being held captive in a tower. (As so often in Spain, the Moors are all-purpose bogeymen; *see* **No Moors are on the coast!**; **Left under the moon of Valencia.**) In due course, a Christian knight-errant rescues Melisendra and whisks her off to Paris, with the Moors in hot pursuit. By this stage, so caught up in the proceedings has the gullible fantasist Don Quixote become that he blunders on set and decapitates the couple's pasteboard pursuers. Not content with this, he then goes berserk and trashes the entire puppet theatre before he can be brought to heel.

This colourful phrase generated no equivalents in other European languages. But such was the success of Cervantes' novel that, within decades of publication, another idiom arising from the book – 'tilting at windmills', from the scene in Part I (Chapter 8), where Quixote charges at windmills on the plain of La Mancha, believing them to be giants – entered into English usage. Even earlier, Don Quixote was responsible for the metaphorical use in English of 'windmill' to signal an airy flight of fancy: after the famous episode, Sancho Panza upbraids his master: 'Didn't I tell your grace ... that these were nothing but windmills, and only somebody whose head was full of windmills wouldn't know that!' Here, Cervantes was apparently employing a common Andalusian expression for a person acting or thinking irrationally. So, in a pleasingly (and aptly) circular way, it seems that the author created a hugely memorable scene from a figurative phrase, only to then have a character use that very phrase to comment on the action.

ASTROTURFING (US)

Describing a popular campaign which looks spontaneous but has in fact been organised, often for political purposes

Here is an ingenious spin-off from the metaphor of grass roots, used to describe the rank-and-file or ordinary supporters of a political party. AstroTurf is the brand name of the artificial grass used to cover sports pitches and the inventive application of the term is credited to a Democratic senator from Texas, Lloyd Bentsen. Commenting in 1985 on a pile of cards and letters he'd received in opposition to an insurance provision which he favoured, Bentsen is supposed to have remarked: 'A fellow from Texas can tell the difference between grass roots and AstroTurf. This is generated mail.' The Texas angle is explained by the fact that AstroTurf takes its name from the synthetic fibre installed at the Astrodome in Houston. At its most manipulative, 'astroturfing' may involve the sending of bogus letters and e-mails by corporations or special interest groups, making it appear that public support for (or opposition to) a particular cause is greater than it really is. There is a fine line, though, between organised protest and the synthetic variety. Samuel Adams, one of the Founding Fathers, was an expert at encouraging rallies against the British and publicising the results in order to encourage other would-be patriots (or rebels). No doubt if the term had existed at the time, his enemies would have accused him of 'astroturfing'.

TO LEAVE IN THE ACE (ITALIAN)
Lasciare/piantare in asso – **to abandon/leave in the lurch**

Ace is an odd word, when you think about it. A single spot or pip on a playing card, or on sets of dice, which by extension has come to mean a uniquely gifted practitioner of his or her art: *a fighter ace, a tennis ace* (also, of course, describing a single, unplayable serve in tennis that wins the point outright). In other words, all positive, approbatory stuff: number one, *nulli secundus*, in a class of one's own.

But as any card player knows, aces can be low as well as high. Here we come to the root of the word: in ancient Rome, the *as* was a bronze (or later, copper) coin of low denomination, worth a quarter of a *sestercius*. As such, it was the most basic unit of Roman currency. In this sense, 'one' signifies not unmatchable excellence, but isolation and loneliness: as in the refrain of the curious English folk song '*Green Grow the Rushes, O*' – 'One is one and all alone/And evermore shall be so'. This, then, is thought to be the most likely derivation of the Italian phrase *lasciare in asso*, which means to suddenly and unexpectedly leave someone on their tod to fend for themselves.

There's an alternative explanation which is worth investigating. According to this, the phrase was originally *lasciare in Nasso*, which over time was elided into its current form. *Nasso* is Italian for Naxos, the island in the Aegean to which the Greek hero Theseus and his helper Ariadne fled after he had slain the minotaur on Crete. Though she, the daughter of King Minos, had provided Theseus with the ball of thread that enabled him to retrace his path out of the labyrinth, he unceremoniously abandoned her on Naxos. An ingenious derivation, but sadly one that is now considered entirely specious by most linguistic authorities.

MONDAY-MORNING QUARTERBACK (US)
Someone who comments on or judges the actions of others with the benefit of hindsight

A quarterback is the player in American football who occupies a position between the linemen and the halfbacks and who is responsible for directing the attack play of his team. The description 'Monday-morning quarterback' refers to someone who, probably in the workplace, dissects and comments critically on the game he has watched over the weekend. The commentator will most likely be amateur in every sense, not letting the lack of qualifications or experience stand in the way of giving a decisive opinion of his own. The phrase, which can also work as a verb, is first recorded as far back as 1931 as 'Sunday morning quarterbacking'. The variant form of 'armchair quarterback' links it with disparaging phrases like 'armchair general' and, more remotely, 'back-seat driver'.

THE WHOLE NINE YARDS (US)
The whole lot, the full package

This expression, first found in print in the 1960s, is the Bermuda Triangle of mysterious idioms, a swallower-up of explanations. Several theories have been advanced as to its source, none of them completely convincing and some highly implausible. The problem arises from the failure of the expression to specify exactly what it is that is being measured in nine yards. At first sight, it might sound like a sporting measurement, and indeed there is a distance which must be travelled in American football to score what is known as a 'first down'. Unfortunately, that distance is ten yards and not nine. The 'yards' component of the expression has also suggested the crosspieces (yardarms) on the masts of a traditional sailing ship. According to this theory, the whole nine yards should describe a ship under full sail. But it is almost impossible that a metaphor which originated in the pre-industrial age of sail should not be recorded in print until the 20th century. A similar objection applies to the notion that it comes from the measure of cloth required to make a three-piece suit. If so – and quite apart from the fact that nine yards of cloth would be almost enough for two suits – why should the expression emerge so late in the day? The date issue is less of a problem if we assume, as some have done, that the nine yards apply to the 27-foot-long ammunition belts used in machine guns during the Second World War; going the 'whole nine yards' would therefore mean using up one's firepower at a single go. Even so, the gap between this possible Second World War source and its earliest citation in print is still an unusually long one.

An out-of-the-way explanation, although one credited by quite a few linguistic investigators, is that the measurement describes the cubic capacity of a cement lorry. This theory suffers from a date problem which is the opposite to the ones mentioned above. Lorries carrying ready-mixed cement before the 1980s had a capacity which was about half of the required nine cubic yards, so this source too seems unlikely. A lighter and more entertaining theory pins the expression on a ribald story involving a Scotsman who loses his kilt, the long scarf which he has knitted for his fiancée, his drunken appearance outside her window one night and a punchline involving 'the whole nine yards'. It *is* possible, of course, that a popular US expression derives from a mildly dirty Scottish joke but no more than (just) possible. Yet another explanation takes us back to the football measurement but with the expression now being intended ironically to describe the player who fails to make the ten-yard run. In this case, one imagines it being expressed in a formula such as: 'Oh yeah, he made the whole nine yards'.

Whatever the mysteries of the source of the 'whole nine yards', it was familiar enough in US parlance to provide the title of a Bruce Willis comedy vehicle in 2000 and – on the principle that no obvious opportunity for a sequel should be wasted – for a follow-up film, *The Whole Ten Yards*. A few years earlier, there appeared the very successful British film, *The Full Monty*, which not only has a similar meaning to the 'whole nine yards' (i.e. 'the whole lot', 'the whole shebang') but, like its American cousin, has provoked much discussion about its obscure origins. (See also **The full Monty**)

GIVE (SOMEONE) A HEADS-UP (US)
Give notice/advance warning

'Heads up!' was an old warning shout given by a look out to alert street traders or gamblers to the imminent arrival of the police. From the 1920s, it turned into an adjective (heads-up) signifying in the United States a state of alertness, particularly in sports. As currently used, the phrase 'giving a heads-up' has a meaning somewhere between providing information and a warning, as in this representative quotation: 'Taylor expected to play Saturday in the pre-season game against the Tennessee

Titans and lamented that he wasn't given more of a "heads up" that he wouldn't, especially because he was in uniform.' (*Chicago Sun-Times*)

The expression obviously derives from a literal call to be on the lookout for some physical danger. The same idea of being alert and focused may lie behind the group injunction from a sports trainer or a military instructor to 'Listen up!', a phrase which is nothing more than an intensified form of 'Listen' but one that seems increasingly popular in British English as well as the American variety.

FISH OR CUT BAIT (US)

Demand that someone choose a specific course of action rather than dither between the two

There is a slight ambiguity to the expression 'fish or cut bait'. On the surface, it is a demand that a person commit himself to a particular course of action. Since you cannot hold a fishing rod and cut (i.e. prepare) bait simultaneously, you must decide which of the two to do. It could be expressed as 'get off the fence'. The metaphorical application of the phrase goes back to the 19th century and can appear in unexpected contexts. A headline in a New York newspaper of May 1915 declared 'Germany Must Fish or Cut Bait'. This 'homely phrase', as it was described, meant that the time for diplomatic fencing was finished following President Wilson's protest at the U-boat sinking of a passenger ship carrying American citizens. But there is a later and more aggressive interpretation of 'fish or cut bait', and it is this which is most commonly meant now. Less 'get off the fence' and more 'put up or shut up'. It is a call for action not words. A blunter and cruder version is 'shit or get off the pot.'

BASEBALL EXPRESSIONS

Cricket has supplied British English with a range of idiomatic expressions from 'hat trick' to 'sticky wicket' and 'a good innings' (when applied to someone's life, this seems to mean dying in or beyond one's mid-eighties). In the United States, baseball has played an equivalent role, providing fertile ground for expressions originating with the game which turn to general metaphors. A handful of the most useful are:

- *left field*: the area on the outer edge of the field to the left, looking from the position of the batter in the centre. At some point during the 1950s, it came to suggest a place that was odd or from which unexpected things might emerge ('All this came from left field. I never planned it.'). It is similar to 'off the wall', another sporting phrase which may derive from the way a squash ball or handball can ricochet unexpectedly from a wall.

- *step up to the plate*: to enter the batter's area for one's turn at batting. This is a baseball moment crying out for figurative treatment, and for many years 'stepping up to the plate' has meant 'taking control' or 'rising to a challenge'. Despite almost universal ignorance of baseball in the United Kingdom, the phrase is surprisingly popular in British English, generally appearing without explanation.

- *ballpark figure:* a rough estimate, an approximate number. Often used in the world of finance to estimate current or future profits, liabilities and so on, the expression may derive from estimating the number of people attending a game. Alternatively, the earlier phrases 'in the ballpark' (within a reasonable range) and 'out of the ballpark' (outside a reasonable range) suggest an assessment based on generally agreed limits, just as a game is played within specific confines.

- *throw a curveball:* to throw a ball, the unexpected trajectory of which, is intended to take the batter by surprise. Like 'out of left field', this characterises anything which arrives unexpectedly and, probably, unwelcomed, since there is a more personal feel to the 'curveball' metaphor especially if the user of the phrase is also the target ('I've made much progress but the least little curveball can still throw me.'). The equivalent in cricket is a 'googly'.

Chapter 3

CORRIDORS OF POWER

We invariably come to loathe those in power, whether we elected them or not. There's a good reason for this; for all their honeyed words about equity and democracy, the only constituency they're truly beholden to is that of the super-wealthy. In return for services rendered, many political cat's-paws get elevated to these dizzy heights themselves (if they didn't start there in the first place, that is). As for the rest of us, their attitude is, and always has been, *oderint dum metuant* – 'let them hate me as long as they fear me'.

The one small, enduring revenge of the Third (or Fourth) Estate is the body of common phrases that are either explicitly disparaging or implicitly convey the popular awareness – born of centuries of bitter experience – that all power corrupts.

US politics is particularly rich in idioms relating to the exercise of power. Perhaps driven by the search for a pithy soundbite, every presidential race seems to throw up a new coinage. Some are marvellously inventive; we need only cite the examples of 'gerrymandering' (19th century) and 'dog-whistle polling' (21st century).

GERRYMANDER (US)

To arrange voting areas in the interests of a particular party; to manipulate circumstances to bring about an unjustifiable or unfair result

This expression, which goes back more than two hundred years, derives from a Governor of Massachusetts, Elbridge

Gerry, who in 1811 signed a bill readjusting the districts in his state so as to favour the Democrats and weaken the opposing Federalist party. An artist, looking at the peculiar shape which resulted on the map, added a head, wings and claws to create the likeness of a salamander, at which point a Boston newspaper editor exclaimed: 'Salamander! Call it a Gerrymander!' The link between manipulating or fiddling boundaries for electoral purposes and Gerry may be slightly unfair since he – one of the signatories to the Declaration of Independence – was apparently reluctant to sign the bill which came to be associated with him. In addition, his name was pronounced with a hard G. But over time the initial letter was softened, probably by association with the pejorative use of 'jerry'[1] as a prefix. The term 'gerrymander', both noun and verb, is widely employed on both sides of the Atlantic, usually about politics but also to describe, say, the structure of a company whose shareholders' voting rights may be rigged to produce a particular outcome.

TO GO WHERE THE KING/QUEEN GOES ALONE (SPANISH)

Ir a donde el rey/la reina va solo – **to powder one's nose/ spend a penny**

Toilets, and their use, have generated a welter of euphemisms. Understandably, people fight shy of calling a spade a spade where bodily functions are concerned. In English,

---

1 Anything 'jerry-built' is poorly constructed while a 'jerry-shop' is a pub. The origins of the negative 'jerry-' are obscure, although suggestions range from the city of Jericho, whose walls came tumbling down, to the name of a Victorian-era builder in Liverpool known for his poor work. The use of 'Jerry' as a slang word for a German dates from the First World War.

circumlocutions range from the boringly overused 'see a man about a dog/horse' to the forced jocularity of 'off to shake hands with the unemployed'. The oddest by far, dating from a time when back-to-back terraced houses had no indoor sanitation and occupants had to dash outside to a brick 'khazi' at the far end of the back yard, is the frankly surreal 'the doughnut in granny's greenhouse'. This formed the punchline to a *Two Ronnies* sketch, in which a man who urgently needs the loo but is too embarrassed to ask straight out, dances round the issue until his interlocutor finally twigs ('Oh, you mean the doughnut...!'). Those arch-pisstakers out of all things prissily British and suburban, The Bonzo Dog Doo-Dah Band, liked it so much that they made it the title of an album released in 1968.

Yet the Spanish phrase harbours its own element of strangeness – after all, doesn't *everyone* go there alone? Until it dawns on you that the life of an absolute monarch was one where privacy was at a premium. Courtiers, ministers, manservants and ladies-in-waiting hovered around you morning, noon and night. The absolutest of them all, the French *Roi-Soleil* Louis XIV, held the first and last audiences of the day (the *lever* and the *coucher*) in his bedchamber. And at the French and English courts, not even the smallest room was sacrosanct: the positions of 'porte-coton' and 'groom of the stool' (instituted by Henry VIII) were much sought after. But not, if we are to believe the idiom, in Spain; perhaps Spanish rulers had a more highly developed sense of personal space.

The prize for the most irritatingly coy expression for the bog must go to the American 'restroom', a term that airbrushes out the titanic effort sometimes exerted within. Certainly (maintaining our royal theme), George II wasn't equal to the struggle; on 25 October 1760, at the then-ripe old age of 77, the second Hanoverian king of Great Britain was found dead at Kensington Palace, having succumbed to a dissecting aneurysm of the aorta while 'straining at stool'. So lending a whole new meaning to the phrase 'succeeding to the throne'.

DOG-WHISTLE ISSUES/POLITICS/ POLLING (US)

The use of coded messages in speeches, electoral polling etc., not for general consumption but designed to be heard by a section of the public

This expression is a relatively recent entrant to the field of political idioms. It derives from the high pitch of a dog-whistle, heard by the animal but not audible to humans. An associated phrase is 'under the radar'. Although the term is new, dog-whistling is a practice that must go back to the days when politicians first had to campaign in public, and discovered they must balance their appeal to some voters against the risk of offending others. Here's an example of how it works. In 1980, Ronald Reagan began his presidential election campaign with an appearance in a town in Missouri near where three young civil rights workers had been murdered in the summer of 1964, a crime that provoked a national outcry and extensive investigation from outside the state. Reagan, who had originally opposed the Civil Rights Act, declared in a speech: 'I believe in states' rights.' The crowds roared their approval, because the candidate was capitalising on long-time resentment against the intrusion of the federal authorities and signalling he was with them. Yet on the surface the remark was innocent, even laudable. In the UK election campaign of 2005, the Conservative Party ran advertisements tagged 'Are You Thinking What We're Thinking?', touching on contentious issues like immigration and the National Health Service, and widely described as dog-whistle politics. The term may have been introduced into Britain by an Australian political consultant involved with the Tory campaign, and it is possible the expression originated there, although there are also examples of American usage from the late 1980s. Because dog-whistle politics deals with sensitive issues, examples of it tend to emanate from right-wing parties: they are aware that explicit comment would alienate centrist voters but nevertheless need to communicate to their core audience that they shares their anxieties.

THIRD RAIL (US)
Highly charged/very dangerous to handle

The surprising thing about this neat metaphor is that it took so long for someone to come up with it. The system of electrification which powers subway trains, involving a current which runs on a third rail alongside the load-bearing ones, dates back to the 1880s. Yet it wasn't until the 1980s that a Democrat Party aide, remembering nightmares he endured as a child from riding the subway system, was inspired to make the memorable comment: 'Social Security is the third rail of American politics. Touch it, you're dead.' Since then, the expression has never looked back. A 'third rail' issue is not only contentious, as areas like affirmative action, smoking bans and so on are contentious, but potentially lethal in electoral terms for a politician to deal with or even sometimes to raise in discussion. In the United States, these issues include any attempt to tighten gun laws, changes to social security and to Medicare, as well as attempts to reach out to countries hitherto regarded as beyond the pale, such as Cuba. In addition to national no-go subjects, individual US states will have their own particular third rail issues, as in this comment from *The Times*: "Farm subsidies are a third rail of Iowa politics," a former staffer on Senator John Edwards's presidential campaign said [...]. "You don't touch them."

A related term, although one with a slightly different meaning, is 'hot button', often used as a hyphenated adjective (hot-button). This applies to an issue that excites strong feelings, both positive and negative. Politicians will use hot-button topics to stir up their core supporters or to undermine their opponents. In the Unites States, almost anything to do with religion or abortion can be employed for its hot-button value. The distinction between this phrase and the third rail is that the latter is potentially fatal while the former is dangerous but, if handled carefully, also very useful. There seems no reason why the third rail expression should not have caught on in Britain where it is equally dangerous to come into contact with a live rail bearing 750 volts, yet it hasn't. The most likely reason is that there are far fewer truly contentious issues in British politics and – race and immigration apart – almost none the mere mention of which will threaten the electoral survival of a politician.

FILIBUSTER (US)

To obstruct legislation (in the US Senate) by speaking continuously

There may not seem to be much of a connection between the swashbuckling world of the pirates of the Spanish Main (in other words, the Caribbean) and the talking heads of the US Senate, but 'filibuster' provides one. It comes originally from a

Dutch expression (*vrijbuiter*) related to 'freebooter'; one who goes after plunder or 'booty'. The word then wound its way through French and Spanish before entering English as 'filibuster'. Its first recorded use in something approaching the modern sense came in 1853 when a senator who had defected because of his own side's support for the forcible annexation of Cuba by the United States – an attempt which he termed 'filibustering' or piracy – was in turn accused by a former colleague of 'filibustering, as I thought, against the United States'. The word rapidly came to define the practice of talking at length to block legislation.

Southern senators opposed to racial equality laws routinely reached for the filibuster, with the record being held by Strom Thurmond, the long-lived South Carolina Senator, who talked for a day and a night (and 18 minutes more) in what was nevertheless a losing battle against the 1957 Civil Rights Act. Relevance didn't matter, since one of Thurmond's many topics included his grandmother's recipe for making biscuits. This archaic, obstructionist procedure has actually been growing in popularity. By one reckoning, the filibuster was used little more than twenty times in the entire 19th century. In the session of Congress between 2007 and 2009, it was employed on more than 60 occasions. The expression and practice soon spread to other English-speaking countries, and it can be applied to any attempt to forestall a vote or a decision by deliberate, long-winded evasion. In the UK parliament, debate may be limited by what's known as a 'guillotine' procedure. The US equivalent is known as a 'cloture vote' (from the French term for 'closure'). Given the curious place filibustering seems to have in the American political psyche, a significant majority is necessary for a cloture vote to succeed.

INSIDE/OUTSIDE THE BELTWAY (US)
Inside/outside the (US) political system

The Beltway is the interstate highway (no. 495) which encircles Washington DC. The term 'beltway' sounds more macho and rugged than the British English 'ring road', although that is what it is. But in its capitalised form, 'Beltway' has a metaphorical application, with political and even glamorous connotations that are entirely lacking in the homely UK equivalent. Because the term is associated with the US centre of power, 'Beltway' hints at a hothouse of prestige, influence, gossip and scandal, a world of supreme concern to those on the inside but diminishing in interest and excitement the further away you get from it.

As a political expression, 'Beltway' may be close to neutral, synonymous with Washington, as in 'the Beltway plan' or 'Beltway lobbyists'. But there is often the suspicion of a sneer – 'the Beltway crowd', 'Beltway culture' – or even outright hostility to the establishment. As a rule, the further to the right the politician, commentator or blogger, the more contemptuous will be any Beltway reference. In this context, the term suggests the insularity, smugness and arrogance of the governing class. It is routine for presidential candidates to incorporate some anti-Beltway digs in their campaigns, promising to change Washington when they get there and do things differently in future, ignoring the fact that they are generally experienced politicos and long-time Beltway insiders themselves.

The nearest UK equivalent is the more cosy-sounding 'Westminster village' which, like 'Beltway', can suggest that there's something both elitist and parochial about power centres. The US usage is occasionally found in a British setting

– as in: 'For inhabitants of the Westminster beltway, life for gay people might appear to have changed completely in recent years' (*Observer*) – which is not only inaccurate, since there is no ring road round Westminster, but also a spurious attempt to catch a bit of Washington glamour.

AXIS OF EVIL (US)

A description of an alliance of countries under repressive rule and with aggressive intentions towards the outside world

It's unusual to pinpoint the emergence of a popular phrase to a single occasion or to be able to attribute it to a single source. But the first public utterance of 'axis of evil' was by US President George W. Bush in his State of the Union address to Congress in January 2002. He was referring to three countries – Iran, Iraq and North Korea – linked by authoritarian leadership and by their aggressive stance towards the outside world. All were, or are thought to be, developing nuclear weapons. The concept of an axis of evil originated with Bush's speechwriter, David Frum, Canadian-born but one of the neo-conservative cabal that was so influential in US policy after 9/11. The expression was originally 'axis of hatred' but another speech writer, senior to Frum, turned 'hatred' into 'evil', presumably because of the more moralistic, even biblical overtones it carries. It was soon pointed out that the principal reason Frum had picked the word 'axis' – because it recalled the Second World War alliance between Germany, Italy and Japan – was more to do with propaganda than fact. Iraq and Iran were never allies, unlike Germany and Italy, and indeed the two countries had fought a bitter and bloody war in the 1980s. Furthermore,

North Korea seemed to have been thrown into the mix to make up the numbers of rogue states.

But as a phrase, 'axis of evil' certainly resonated. Opponents of Bush's foreign policy claimed that it showed his simplistic, even Manichean world view. Supporters applauded his candour. David Frum's wife proudly outed her husband as the originator of an expression which duly acquired an edgy popularity and some punning spin-offs. 'Axis of the willing' described those countries which were prepared to stand alongside the US in the 2003 invasion of Iraq, while 'axis of weasels' characterised those countries which weren't ready to join in. 'Axles of evil' was connected to the environmental impact of SUVs, 'axis of weevil' with genetically modified crops. And so on.

'- GATE' (US)

Suffix attached to another word, frequently a name, and denoting a scandal

It took only a day or two in the midsummer of 2011 for an unwisely tweeted photo of a US congressman's crotch (in underpants), sent to a woman who was following him on Twitter, to become known as 'Weinergate'. For Anthony Weiner, the representative of one of New York's districts, it was the end of a promising career, his plight not helped by the fact that his surname is uncomfortably close to 'wiener', US slang for the penis. (Literally, the German adjective *Wiener* means 'from Vienna' but in the compound form of *Wienerwurst* it describes a small sausage and so inevitably leads to the slang sense.)

All such '-gate' terms – and there are hundreds – go back to original Watergate scandal of 1974, when an attempted burglary at the Democratic Party headquarters in the riverside Watergate building in Washington DC was linked to the 1972 campaign to re-elect President Richard Nixon. Although it was the subsequent cover-up rather than the break-in that caused Nixon's 1974 resignation, the Watergate effect was so dramatic and far-reaching that the suffix '-gate' has been added ever since to any scandal, particularly when it threatens the reputation of a public figure. The term has even spread to non-English-speaking countries like Germany and Greece. By origin, 'watergate' is a blameless Middle English word, describing a gate opening onto water or a place through which water traffic passes. *The Oxford Dictionary of American Political Slang* (2004) lists over a hundred '-gate' expressions and there are many more on Wikipedia. In the case of Congressman Weiner, the '-gate' suffix might have been justified, since it was an authentic if minor political scandal. Some of the other applications of this term are absurd, however, and many are strained, as the media reach for a hand-me-down expression to signify any hint of impropriety or wrong-doing. In fact, the overuse of '-gate' is so flagrant and shameless that one might talk of a Gate-gate.

PASS THE BUCK (US)

To transfer blame or shift responsibility to somebody else

This expression originated as a piece of American gaming slang. Mark Twain uses it in his comic narrative *Roughing It* (1872) during an encounter between a minister of religion and a fireman, who wants to make funeral arrangements for a friend (coincidentally or otherwise called Buck). The minister's high-flown language is not understood by the fireman, who says: 'You ruther hold over me, pard. I reckon I can't call that hand. Ante and pass the buck.' In effect, the speaker means, 'let's start again'. The link with 'ante' (to stake or to pay up) shows that the expression derives from poker. During a game, a 'buck' or marker was passed to signify a change of dealer. The only slight mystery hangs over the nature of the buck, a word with multiple meanings. Candidates include a piece of buckshot (the large shot used in shooting deer), the slang term for a dollar (the so-called silver dollar coin or 'buck'[2]) or a shortened form of 'buckhorn' (a buck's horn could be used to make knife handles).

Of these sources the most likely is the last, and the image of a buckhorn knife being passed around the gaming table is appropriate to the Wild West context of the term even if it has been remarked that having a weapon so readily to hand might have sharpened the risk of a dispute turning serious. In the early part of the 20th century, the expression took on its current sense of shifting responsibility and even blame. The famous variant 'the buck stops here', claiming ultimate responsibility rather than passing it on, was popularised by Harry S. Truman, the US President between 1945 and 1953, who kept a sign with that phrase on his desk in the Oval Office. Truman did not originate this form of the expression but it has remained popular with presidents ever since, as well as those critics who like to point out that the buck stops at the White House.

---

2 The origin of 'buck' to signify a dollar is not clear. It may come from the use of a dollar coin as an alternative marker in poker to a buckhorn knife, with the knife expression being transferred to the currency. An alternative and older source dates it to the days of early American settlement (by Europeans) when the skins of bucks and does were used as a money substitute in transactions.

HOW WILL IT PLAY IN PEORIA? (US)

How will this proposal, plan or product be received by an averagely critical audience or market?

Peoria is a town in the state of Illinois, about 100 miles south-west of Chicago. Because of its size, midwestern location and the demographic make-up of its population, Peoria was long regarded as representative of 'typical' American opinion away from the distorting pressures of the capital or big cities. In 1969, during Richard Nixon's stint in the White House, a member of his inner circle was asked why the President had made a certain move that was provoking criticism in Washington. 'Don't worry,' was the reply. 'It'll play in Peoria.' The aide, John D. Ehrlichman (later to be imprisoned for his role in the Watergate affair), was mistakenly credited with coining the Peoria phrase, but in fact it dates back at least to the early 20th century. Any assumptions that the town stands for the provincial or the hick are also misplaced since Peoria, although not a metropolitan centre, had a reputation during the days of vaudeville as one of the toughest towns in which to get a laugh. If a new act or comic turn went down well there, it could be successful anywhere. Subsequently, 'Will it play in Peoria?' became a catchphrase on radio programmes in the 1930s.

The expression is still alive and well in the United States, even though Peoria may no longer be demographically typical of contemporary America. The 'playing in Peoria' phrase does, however, answer the need to pinpoint the most average spot in a country in order for a market researcher or a pollster to test out new ideas and products. A number of English towns might be candidates for such a role but, in a more compact country, commentators tend to fall back on the expression 'middle England'. (see also **Nascar Dad**)

BOONDOGGLE (US)

(as verb) to do work which has no real value;
(as noun) a project which is lavish but pointless

This odd and amateur-sounding word, which is not found in British English, has an odd derivation. It appears to describe a piece of braided leather, either the lanyard worn by Boy Scouts or an ornamental addition to a saddle. According to a 1935 report in the *Chicago Tribune*, cowboys 'boondoggled when there was nothing else to do on the ranch', meaning that they spent their time making saddle decorations out of spare scraps of leather. From this harmless (if not very useful) activity comes the contemporary use of the term, more often found as a noun than a verb and always pejorative in application. A 'boondoggle' is a waste of money on a grand scale ostensibly in pursuit of some government programme, as suggested by such newspaper headlines as 'The Pentagon's Biggest Boondoggles'. It has something in common with the widely used 'pork/pork barrel' to characterise government programmes and projects that may bring financial benefit to a few but which do not have any real useful application. And the word may have a wider meaning to indicate sharp practice or, at the least, something which is not straightforward, as in this humorous definition from the *Los Angeles Times*: 'Boondoogle – Business trip whose location is chosen for travel/vacation motives.'

LIKE KING CHARLEMAGNE/
CHARLES (ITALIAN)

Alla carlona – **in a slapdash/slovenly way, carelessly**

Across northern Italy (southerners use a different expression, *alla sanfrason*), this phrase is used pejoratively, in such contexts as *Un lavoro fatto alla carlona* – a 'rush job'. Even by extension, as in the Ligurian braised rabbit dish *coniglio alla carlona*, the connotation is of something quickly rustled up, involving no real effort. But how did Charlemagne (742–814) – king of the Franks and the first Holy Roman Emperor, who consolidated his power throughout Western Europe and is widely seen as wise and humane – come to be synonymous with carelessness and neglect?

Its provenance is sketchy. One suggested explanation is that, in the medieval Old French epic poems recounting the Carolingian legends, the *chansons de geste*, Charlemagne often appears as good-natured but lacking any shrewdness or guile. This reputation for fecklessness may ultimately rest on his failure to secure the succession. The Frankish custom of apportioning lands among all male heirs of a ruler (as opposed to the usual practice of primogeniture) meant that the empire fell apart soon after his death, fragmented by bitter rivalries.

Yet the phrase seems to have become current only in the 16th century. Given that *alla carlona* actually only means 'in the manner of Carlo [= Charles]', maybe Charlemagne isn't the intended target after all. A closer match in terms of both time and temperament is Charles VIII, king of France from 1483 to 1498, whose invasion of Italy in 1494 sparked a long series of Franco-Italian wars. Defeated by the League of Venice the following year, he withdrew in disarray, losing all of his gains and most of his army. This ill-conceived adventure not only laid waste the peninsula (Florence and Viterbo were ransacked by Charles' Swiss mercenaries, along with several other smaller towns) but also left France sunk in debt and politically unstable.

Charles VIII would be a far more fitting symbol of recklessness and disorder than poor old Carolus Magnus. Who knows? Not for the first time in the murky world of idiom sources, take your pick…

TO GO FROM HEROD TO PILATE (Spanish)

Ir de Herodes a Pilatos – **to go from pillar to post/be sent all round the houses**

The Gospel of St Luke, Chapter 23, verses 6–11, recounts how Christ, after his arrest, was sent first to Pontius Pilate, the Roman governor of Judea, and thence to Herod Antipas (the Roman client ruler of Galilee, in whose territory Jesus had been active), and finally back to Pilate once more. It was clear that the authorities were at a loss at what do to with this charismatic troublemaker.

In Spanish, the image of Christ being passed from one jurisdiction to another expresses the frustration of being sent on a wild goose chase. It can be used in any context, but is strongly associated with the soul-sapping business of negotiating unhelpful officialdom.

German has almost the same idiom, with the same meaning, but adds an interesting twist: *Von Pontius zu Pilatus laufen*. It clearly has something of the alliterative punch of the English 'pillar to post' (originally 'post to pillar', origin unknown), but beyond this also emphasises the utter fruitlessness of the enterprise. Not to mention the sheer absurdity of shuttling between two parts of a single person's name. We're in the realm of Franz Kafka's most famous characters here, K. and Josef K., who (in the novels *The Castle* and *The Trial* respectively) spend their lives trying to penetrate the endless concentric circles of a nightmarish bureaucracy.

ROME IN METAPHORS

As the most powerful city in the ancient world and the seat of the papacy ever since, Rome has always been a model, an inspiration – and a gift to phrase makers.

- *Rome wasn't built in a day*: great achievements and large tasks take time and effort to accomplish. Both a warning against haste and a consolation to those making slow progress, this expression has existed in English since at least the 16th century.

- *All roads lead to Rome*: although there may appear to be many routes and directions, they all ultimately lead to the same central point. Or, there are several ways of accomplishing the same goal (close in meaning to the old proverbial saying that 'there's more than one way to skin a cat').

- *Fiddling while Rome burns*: to be engaged in some insignificant and distracting activity while a much more important event is taking place, with the implication that the 'fiddle-player' actually has the power to do something to mitigate the effects of the real crisis. The reference is to what is more of a legend or rumour than an accredited historical fact: that the Emperor Nero played the lyre as Rome was burning down around him.

Chapter 4

GASTRONOMIC DELIGHTS

It may simply be that people who are obsessed with words, like the present authors, have an oral fixation, but we would submit that there's a strong affinity between the gustatory pleasure of eating and the linguistic pleasure afforded by a juicy idiom. After all, aren't both a kind of *amuse-bouche*? To forego the delight of lacing your speech with these tasty morsels is to be like those poor wretches who take a purely utilitarian attitude to food, treating it as mere fuel. And, just as true gourmands will find their palate tickled by exotic tastes from other cuisines, so the pleasure of idioms only increases if you master them in foreign languages, too.

Here, then, for your delectation is our *smörgåsbord* of food and drink idioms, featuring not only familiar dishes such as cold turkey, apple pie and artichoke, but also far less digestible items like grass snakes, rabid cows and a monkey sandwich. Enjoy!

TO HAVE THE HEART OF AN ARTICHOKE
(FRENCH)

Avoir un coeur d'artichaut – **to be fickle in love**

This is a delightfully whimsical idiom, encapsulating both the French love of food and their often refreshingly playful take on affairs of the heart. It is thought to date from the late 19th century, and alludes to the classic way of eating globe artichokes, boiled and served with a vinaigrette or hollandaise sauce. A large choke – and some do grow very large indeed – can be shared by a group of diners, each person tugging off the individual leaves and nibbling at the edible bases. So, to have the heart of an artichoke is to peel off your affections, one by one, and distribute them to all and sundry.

A 19th-century food writer, E. S. Dallas (quoted in Jane Grigson's *Vegetable Book*), drew a different lesson from the artichoke: 'It is good for a man to eat thistles,' he wrote, 'and to remember that he is an ass.'

EAT CROW (US)

Own up to being wrong about some matter and experience mild humiliation as a result

The expression 'eating crow', which appeared in the United States in the 1850s and which is still very much in use, looks as though it belongs to that small family of phrases signifying humiliation after being proved wrong and turning on the idea of swallowing something unpleasant or indigestible, as in 'eat one's hat' or 'eat dirt'. To literally eat crow is presumably a disagreeable experience even if you don't have to do it raw (the original expression was 'eating boiled crow'). But the chances are that the phrase has nothing to do with the bird.

In the 17th century, the word 'crow', in addition to its other meanings, described part of an animal's intestines. (This alimentary sense derives from old German or Dutch, while the bird-sense comes from Old English.) A different and early term for animal intestines – usually a deer's innards – is the Middle English *umbles* or *numbles*. These relatively unvalued parts of the animal could be eaten in the form of an 'umble pie', although it wouldn't have been a top-table dish. The shift from eating an umble pie to eating 'humble pie' is the shift from the literal to the metaphoric, and it is first noted in its modern 'humiliated' sense in English as late as 1830.

The link between 'humble' in the sense of 'meek' and umbles/ numbles/humbles signifying a deer's guts is a link of sound alone. But it's ripe for a pun since those who were low-born or had been brought low would be more likely to consume a pie made of umbles. Only a few years separate the first recorded metaphorical uses of eating humble pie in Britain and eating crow in the United States, although both terms were probably in oral circulation before that. They eat humble pie as well as crow in America but it is tempting to speculate that, rather than indicating the bird, 'crow' here refers to the intestines. If so, it is an example of an old linguistic usage which the early settlers carried with them across the Atlantic.

'RAILWAY EMBANKMENT' BRAND (GERMAN)
Marke Bahndamm – **rot-gut/poor quality (e.g. tobacco, wine)**

From its inception in the 1830s, the railway became not only a driving force behind industrial growth but also – through the greater mobility it suddenly offered people – a prime mover for social change. At the same time, the economics of railway construction required that it cross only the most unfavoured tracts of land when entering towns. And following its arrival, property built close to its course was bound to be either strictly utilitarian or, if residential, of the meanest and lowliest kind. So it was that the railway became a marker of social status: the hangdog curmudgeon Tony Hancock lived at the downmarket address of 23 Railway Cuttings, East Cheam, while the US phrase 'from the wrong side of the tracks' described someone who couldn't afford to escape a life spent downwind of the constant soot, smoke and noise of locomotives.

Likewise, anything that thrives along railway embankments or cuttings is by definition the poor relation of the plant kingdom – a straggly, invasive weed. Think of the swathes of rosebay willowherb and buddleia that fringe Britain's railway tracks, their seeds spread by the wind and the suction of passing trains. And so to our German idiom: easy to imagine the hacksaw rasp in your throat after inhaling the smoke of tobacco that tastes as if it had been cultivated on such terrain. Winegrowers then adopted the term, using it to describe shaded slopes with poor soil that produced a lower yield than other plots in the vineyard.

Another term in German for a fierce, tar-packed fag that pulls no punches is the gloriously graphic *Lungentorpedo*. This is commonly applied to the 'Roth-Händle' ('Little Red Hand') brand, the German hard-nut smoker's equivalent of the untipped 'Player's Navy Cut' or 'Capstan Full Strength'. A popular gallows-humour rhyming couplet runs:

Siehst Du den Toten am Straßenrand?
Der war auch Raucher Roter Hand.
['See that stiff in the gutter, gazing at you?
He was a Red Hand smoker, too.']

COME THE RAW PRAWN   (Australian)
To try to deceive/put one over

Like some other Australian expressions, 'come the raw prawn' is colourful, bizarre and slightly obscure in its origins. 'Prawn' has long been used in English to signify somebody foolish and insignificant (compare with a similar use of 'shrimp'). This sense may be reinforced by the echo of 'pawn' in the word. 'Prawnhead' has been Australian slang for a fool since the 1960s. A *literal* raw prawn is something which is hard to swallow – even if it may be presented as a delicacy in Japan – and so by metaphorical extension the term is applied to an attempt to deceive. To 'come the raw prawn' is to try to trick a person or to treat someone as being a gullible individual.

MONKEY SANDWICH STORY (Dutch)
Broodje aap verhaal – **an urban myth**

We're all familiar with urban legends or urban myths – pieces of amusing hokum, majoring on the macabre, which are peddled as true stories. The Internet, a happy hunting ground for hoaxers and conspiracy theorists, is now a polytunnel for their propagation. One of the best of recent years was 'The Accidental Tourist'. A backpacker in a beanie hat is seen posing for a snap on the rooftop observation deck of the North Tower of the World Trade Center at 8.45 on the morning of 11 September 2001. Behind him, against the sunlit backdrop of Manhattan, looms the ominous silver shape of American Airlines Flight 11, seconds before impact. Several crass errors soon saw the picture exposed as a deft bit of Photoshoppery, but it refused to go quietly. Instead, ever cruder cut-outs of the hapless bloke began to pop up, *Zelig*-like, in front of famous disasters of the past, including the *Concorde* crash in Paris, the *Hindenburg* fire and the departure of the *Titanic* on her maiden voyage. An urban myth that morphed into a running visual gag.

The English term 'urban myth' really doesn't do justice to such inventive nonsense. The lurid Dutch phrase *Broodje aap verhaal*, on the other hand, nails the essential *Grand Guignol* of the genre. And it has a clear provenance. In 1978, the Dutch-Jewish writer Ethel Portnoy (1927–2004), a native of Philadelphia who emigrated to Holland in 1951, published *Broodje aap: De Folklore van de Post-Industriele Samenleving*

('Monkey Sandwich: The Folklore of Post-Industrial Society'). In it, she documented various tall tales she'd collected in the United States, England and France. The title story, from the Bronx, recounts how the ghastly 'truth' about New York's ubiquitous hot dogs supposedly came to light after two delivery trucks collided outside the factory making them, disgorging the body parts of gorillas, bears and monkeys from the nearby zoo.

Ironically, the actual content of a hot dog (an unappetizing slurry known as 'mechanically recovered meat' or MRM, which is obtained by hosing down carcasses with high-pressure jets) is liable to do you far more harm than any prime cut of wild beast. As food became ever scarcer during the siege of Paris in the Franco-Prussian War of 1870–71, the inhabitants of the city's zoo, including two elephants named Castor and Pollux, were butchered and eaten. A restaurant menu for Christmas Day 1870 offered the desperate gourmet such delicacies as kangaroo stew, antelope terrine and haunch of wolf. Interestingly (post-Darwin), the monkeys and the great apes of the Paris zoo were thought to be too close to humans, and so were spared the chop.

TO BE OUT OF ONE'S PLATE (FRENCH)

Ne pas être dans son assiette – **to be out of sorts, under the weather**

As dining habits grew more genteel, the communal dipping of hands into a single large tureen was superseded by crockery and cutlery. Forks, for instance (at this stage, still with just two tines), were popularised in Europe by the French king Henri III (r.1574–89). This new-fangled mode of eating was shunned by virile, aristocratic trenchermen of the period as impossibly effete – Henri's court was widely reputed to be a hotbed of homosexuality – but the future ultimately belonged to individual eating irons and plates.

At first, *assiette*, which is cognate with the verb *s'asseoir* (to sit down), simply meant 'place', 'position', 'posture', or 'bearing'. This sense persists in some specialised contexts. For example, a now slightly archaic way of describing the 'attitude' of an aircraft (i.e. its orientation in a horizontal plane) was *l'assiette d'un avion*. Likewise, in a dining context, it originally denoted a place allocated to an individual at table and, by extension, their place setting. From there, it was a short step for the word to take on the figurative sense of 'disposition' or 'demeanour'. In general usage, though, it came increasingly to signify a plate.

So, to be described as not being in your place/plate meant that you weren't in your familiar state of mind. A similar notion of psychological displacement is conveyed in the English term 'to be beside oneself' and its German equivalent *außer sich sein*.

LAST CHANCE SALOON (US/UK)

Signifying a final opportunity to make reforms or get something done after which the situation will deteriorate

This US phrase is surprisingly popular in Britain. It originated in 19th century America where it was used as a combination of enticement and threat. Travellers crossing from one legal jurisdiction to another and entering an area where alcohol was not readily available, or even prohibited altogether, either took the opportunity for a drink at the last-chance saloon or went thirsty. To ensure the point was not missed, the phrase was often used for the name of the bar or tavern itself.

In the United Kingdom – a country lacking alcohol-free areas – the last chance saloon is both metaphorical and widespread. It can be applied to almost any situation: reform of intrusive press practices; climate-change talks; IVF treatment for infertile couples; investment opportunities; or even a visit to a rehab clinic. The existence of a particular type of car in the UK was tailor-made for punning headlines like: 'Last chance saloon for family motors'. But the most fertile soil for the last chance saloon is sport. Whether it's a team captain who's disgraced himself, a team on the verge of relegation or a national application to host the World Cup, the last chance saloon is large enough to contain them all. The sporting context also encourages strained elaboration of the metaphor, as in 'Halifax were said to be drinking in the Last Chance Saloon before this match, in which case last orders have been called and the doors are slamming shut' (*The Times*). The association between sport and frantic drinking may seem odd at first but, apart from the fact that alcohol often features somewhere in sporting misbehaviour, there is a faint but unmistakable macho tang to having a metaphorical drink in the last chance saloon. After all, the drinker's next step is across the boundary, into the unknown desert of dry territory.

TO SWALLOW GRASS SNAKES (FRENCH)

Avaler les couleuvres – **to suffer humiliation in silence/ believe everything you're told**

Traditionally the French have delighted, like Joyce's Mr Leopold Bloom, in eating the inner organs of beasts and fowls. Offal treats alien to (Southern) English palates appear on their menus such as pigs' intestines (in the regional sausage delicacy known as *andouillette* – once accurately described as 'guts in a condom') and calves' pancreas (*ris de veau*). This idiom, though, suggests that there are at least some things that disgust the Gallic gastronome.

Couleuvre (Engl. 'colubrid') is a term for non-venomous snakes in general, but most commonly means 'grass snake'. *Avaler les couleuvres* in its first figurative sense dates back to at least the 17th century, when it was used by the diarist Madame de Sévigné to describe the humiliations meted out to an acquaintance's lover. In subsequent centuries, Chateaubriand and Stendhal employed it in a similar vein.

But why this food item in particular? Claude Duneton's anthology of French idioms, *La Puce à l'oreille*, provides a convincing explanation. In the days when eels were widely eaten, hosts wishing to avenge themselves on someone, or simply given to practical joking, may have slipped the odd unpalatable (and very similar-looking) grass snake into the dish to test their guests' forbearance. Etiquette demanded that you didn't kick up a fuss.

It's a short step from this sense of 'taking what you're given without demur' to the idea of swallowing everything that's served up to you (i.e. being credulous). This is invariably the force of the phrase in modern French.

DRINK THE KOOL-AID (US)
To display blind obedience/accept an argument or course of action without protest and even with enthusiasm

In November 1978, more than 900 members of a cultish pseudo-religion known as the People's Temple, committed suicide in Jonestown in Guyana, by swallowing a powdered drink preparation which was probably Kool-Aid but which was undeniably laced with cyanide. The victims were followers of Jim Jones, the founder of the Temple and a self-proclaimed revolutionary messiah. The mass suicides took place after the murder of a US Congressman who was investigating human rights abuses at the Jonestown settlement. Although the deaths were largely voluntary, they seemed to have occurred because of the delusional mindset which Jones encouraged in his followers. The scale of the event – the greatest number of civilian deaths to occur in a single non-natural disaster before the 9/11 attack – stunned the American public. Early references to 'drinking the Kool-Aid' tended to focus on the suicidally destructive overtones of the action, but enough time has passed for the expression to be used as a metaphor for obedience and acceptance, without (much) risk of the user being accused of tastelessness. Even so, the phrase has a rough edge which makes it more appropriate for off-the-cuff spoken remarks or in blogs and online publications, as in: *We should all stop drinking the Kool-Aid on China, and that includes China itself.*[1] *Anyone can drink the Kool-Aid, but to dump on your own employer requires a certain degree of both self-awareness and (hopefully) honesty.*[2]

TO PLAY THE INSULTED LIVER SAUSAGE
(GERMAN)

Die beleidigte Leberwurst spielen – **to get in a huff/go off in a sulk**

Ancient medical sources such as the Egyptian Ebers Papyrus (1500 BC) and the writings of the Roman physician Galen (AD 129–199) identified the liver as the seat of human

1 'G20: Stop taking the China Kool-Aid'. 2 April 2009. http://blogs.telegraph. co.uk/news/richardspencer/9362723/G20_Stop_taking_the_China_KoolAid/
2 'Fearless Feedback! Tech Workers Dish Dirt on Their Employers'. 17 July 2009. http://www1.salon.com/tech/giga_am/tech_insider/2009/07/17/ fearless_feedback_tech_workers_dish_dirt_on_their_employers/index.html

emotions, especially anger. This is generally thought to be the source of this seemingly peculiar idiom. Sound reasoning indeed, corroborated by the phrase *frisch von der Leber weg reden* (literally 'to talk straight from the liver,' meaning to speak one's mind without inhibition).

Since there's something inherently silly about sausages, the *Wurst* element was presumably added to heap mockery on the sulker. In an example of what anthropologists call an 'aetiological myth', Upper Saxon folklore later concocted a story to explain the origin of the phrase: after slaughtering a pig, a butcher began preparing sausages of various kinds from its innards. He lifted the black puddings, which need less cooking time, out of the boiling water first; on seeing this, the liver sausage, jealous and resentful at being left to stew, burst its skin.

BETWEEN THE PEAR AND THE CHEESE
(FRENCH)

Entre la poire et le fromage – **casual/off the record/in confidence/unguarded**

A foreigner eating for the first time at a restaurant or with friends in France might be surprised to be offered cheese before dessert. But dining *à la française* wasn't always like that, at least not if we're to believe this idiom. In the medieval period whence it originates, the wealthy few who indulged in formal dinners – with their heavy emphasis on meat, and an attendant paucity of vegetables – are believed to have cleansed their palates with fruit before the cheeseboard.

Then again, in his fascinating study *Cheese, Pears, and History in a Proverb* (Columbia University Press, 2010), Massimo Montanari has traced the idiom to a rhyming couplet that only works if the cheese precedes the pear: '*Entre le fromage et la poire/Chacun dit sa chanson à boire'* ('Between the cheese and the pear/Everyone sings his own drinking song.')

Whatever the running order of the courses, though, the force of the phrase is the same. Between the pear/cheese – or cheese/pear – was the time when drinking began and guests could relax and chat freely. (Contrary to the Hollywood image of Charles Laughton as Henry VIII quaffing sack and banqueting, it appears that most drinking in the Middle Ages was done after, and not during, meals.) And so this juncture of proceedings became a proverbial expression for a relaxed atmosphere where you could horse-trade, cajole and persuade. Maybe even let your tongue become a little too loose; the idiom may also have the nuance of 'saying something (you later regret) in an unguarded moment'. The medieval equivalent of Facebook.

COLD TURKEY (US)
A sudden withdrawal from an addiction

Going 'cold turkey' began as a reference to withdrawal from hard-drug addiction but has spread to encompass giving up almost any form of addictive behaviour such as smoking, compulsive texting, fondness for chocolate etc. The key elements are the abruptness of the attempt to break the addiction, and the unpleasant symptoms which result – 'Temperature's rising/Fever is high' is the opening of John Lennon's 1969 song titled 'Cold Turkey'. There is no certain explanation for the origin of the term, which is first recorded in the 1920s, and several suggestions have been given. To begin with the least likely, they are:

a) providing a meal of literal cold turkey doesn't require much preparation. In the same way, the addict is served up the metaphorical cold turkey treatment without preparation.

b) cold turkey is the main ingredient in the leftovers dished up after Thanksgiving and Christmas. It marks the comedown from a period of indulgence; a return to reality.

c) the phrase is a spin-off from another US idiom, 'to talk turkey', originally meaning 'to talk affably', and then changing into its near-opposite, 'to speak bluntly', 'to talk business'. A development of the first phrase, 'talking cold turkey', had this sense in the 19th century, and it is possible that the idea of direct, uncomfortable speech was connected to the harsh treatment which the addict needed to break free of addiction.

d) some of the physical symptoms of drug withdrawal – coldness, sweating, pimpled skin – are like plucked but uncooked turkey flesh. If we need a reliable authority for this, John Lennon's lyrics also contain a reference to 'goose-pimple bone'.

As with many idioms, the source of 'cold turkey' will never be established for certain, but explanation d), perhaps with a dash of c), seems the most likely.

EAT THE RABID COW (FRENCH)

Manger/bouffer de la vache enragée – **to be on the breadline/ live from hand to mouth**

This isn't some sly dig at English eating habits under the shadow of BSE[3], as it turns out, but a phrase originating in the

---

3 In fact, the French for 'mad cow' is *la vache folle*. Neither this nor *la vache enragée* should be confused with *La Vache Qui Rit*, a processed cheese sold in English-speaking countries as 'The Laughing Cow' (though some would argue you'd have to be just as desperate to eat that).

18th century (or maybe even earlier) and denoting a parlous state in which a person is reduced to consuming diseased meat.

Victor Hugo popularised the idiom when he described characters in his 1862 novel *Les Misérables* in these terms, but perhaps its most intriguing usage came 20–30 years later. In 1885, the writer Émile Goudeau published a novel entitled *La Vache Enragée* about a struggling painter in Montmartre. In 1896–97, a group of Bohemian artists from this run-down district, led by the illustrator and political satirist Adolphe Willette, organised the *Fête de la Vache Enragée*, a parody of the traditional Mardi Gras celebration (*Fête du Boeuf Gras*) held on Shrove Tuesday. The highlight of the alternative, antiestablishment festival was a parade (*la vachalcade*) through the streets of Montmartre. They also published the monthly *Journal de la Vache Enragée*, a compilation of poems and drawings. Contributors included Henri de Toulouse-Lautrec, who in the magazine's first year submitted a lithograph showing a whey-faced, panic-stricken bourgeois waving aloft his umbrella and running hell-for-leather to save himself from being gored by the crazed bovine.

George Orwell's 1933 work *Down and Out in Paris and London* was translated into French two years later, by R. N. Raimbault and Gwen Gilbert, as *La Vache Enragée*. A nicely pithy and apposite title for this account of the author's exploits as a *plongeur* plumbing the depths (and the sinks) of squalid restaurant kitchens.

A French native speaker, writing in a forum on the excellent WordReference.com translation website, suggests that this phrase is now rather old hat in this sense and that *Manger de la vache enragée* is now increasingly being used to describe an aggressive person. What a shame – the original was much more richly allusive...

COLD SHOULDER (UK)
To slight/be aloof towards

A colourful but false story has been attached to giving someone the cold shoulder. It's suggested that a host in the medieval period who didn't think much of a particular visitor would offer him a cold shoulder of mutton. No doubt the guest would be sent off to gnaw away at the meat in the coldest corner of the baronial hall. Unfortunately for this neat theory, the expression does not appear in print until 1816 when Sir Walter Scott used it in his novel *The Antiquary*. Scott took the trouble to define the phrase in a glossary to the novel ('to appear cold and reserved'), showing that it would not be familiar to his readers. The idiom, which has never looked back since Scott's day, almost certainly derives from the simple bodily motion of turning away from someone to demonstrate indifference or dislike. One could even see it as the metaphorical and emotional counterpart of providing a shoulder to cry on.

A related idiom is 'sending to Coventry' but, if giving the cold shoulder denotes a slight or a dismissal, the Coventry process is more like being pushed into the deep freeze. It is a communal punishment for a person who has infringed some rule, and entails a refusal to speak to that person or even to acknowledge his or her existence. Some early references indicate that it was used among army officers or in the hunting fraternity, while the practice was occasionally employed in British industrial disputes in the 1960s when workers who had fallen foul of their union might be sent to Coventry by their workmates. The origin is obscure. It may derive from the English Civil War and the sending of captured Royalist prisoners to Coventry, which was a parliamentary stronghold. Presumably, the prisoners would not have been warmly received.

PORK BARREL (US)

Central government funding for projects which benefit a particular region and which therefore boost the popularity of the incumbent politician and may help in his or her re-election

Like many metaphorical expressions, the precise origins of the 'pork barrel' are obscure even if the literal image of a tubful of fatty meat is plain enough. It may simply refer to the barrel of salted pork which a household kept in the larder in the pre-freezer era, the fullness of which would be a measure of domestic prosperity. More likely there is an allusion to the pre-Civil War practice of making slaves vie with each other for their share in rations of pork. The metaphorical application, frequently shortened to 'pork', has been used in the United States in a negative way since the 1870s and serves as shorthand for routine condemnations of federal extravagance, favouritism and even corruption – at least for those not in receipt of the pork barrel projects. The waste or misuse of federal funds is frequently summed up in the various 'bridge to nowhere' projects. The most flagrant of these was a proposed bridge in Alaska, which would have been nearly as long as the Golden Gate Bridge and higher than the Brooklyn Bridge, connecting an island of 50 inhabitants to the mainland. To date, it has not been built.

The blurred quality of the 'pork barrel' phrase is a reminder of humanity's ambivalent view of pigs (remember Winston Churchill's remark that 'a pig will look a man in the eye and see his equal'). It is not only the pork barrel schemes which are tainted or greasy, wasteful or fatty. It is also the human beings, motivated by greed and self-interest, who stick their arms – or snouts – into the barrel. An alternative (and less harsh) US expression for the pork barrel is 'earmarks', designating funds which are to be employed on a particular project. Pork barrel projects can also be linked to another wood-related metaphor, that of 'log-rolling'. In its literal sense, this looks back to the pioneering days of American settlement and describes the mutual help given by neighbours when land had to be cleared and wood shifted. It soon acquired a less innocent interpretation, indicated by the proverbial saying 'You roll my log and I'll roll yours'. In the political sphere, log-rolling suggests not so much mutual help as a cynical, even corrupt, exchange of favours. The expression also occurs in the literary world, where mutual back-scratching among writers/ reviewers is not unknown, especially in the books-of-the-year Christmas features. (See also **Boondoggle**)

APPLE-PIE ORDER (UK/US?)
Neat/well organised

There is no general agreement about the origin of the homely phrase 'apple-pie order', which is first recorded towards the end of the 18th century. One theory holds that it is a corruption (i.e. a usage distorted by time and error) of the French *nappes pliés* or 'folded linen'. An alternative suggestion for a French source is that it is a mangled version of the formula phrase *cap-à-pie*, at one time used in English with the meaning of 'head to toe' (the ghost of Hamlet's father is described as appearing in armour 'cap-a-pe') or 'top to bottom'. There is no firm evidence linking 'apple-pie order' with either of these, and in the case of the second it seems an uncomfortable leap from a phrase with distinctly military overtones to one that generally evokes a domestic kind of neatness. A third 'corrupt' derivation is from a slurring of the first two letters of the Greek alphabet (alpha, beta), in which case 'apple-pie' simply means as orderly as the alphabet. Yet another possibility, perhaps suggested by phrases such as 'motherhood and apple pie' or 'as American as apple-pie', makes the connection with the way the traditional New England housewife cut apples into even slices before placing them row upon neat row in the pie dish.

A NATIONAL OBSESSION

The French love of eating has become something of a cliché, especially when seen through the eyes of their Northern European neighbours: the films *Babette's Feast* (1987) and *Chocolat* (2000), based on books by a Danish and British writer respectively, are relatively recent examples. But like all clichés, it's built on the bedrock of truth. The central role played by food in French culture finds expression in the sheer number and diversity of food-related idioms in the language.

Sure, some are simple equivalents of foodie phrases in English or other languages: e.g. *se vendre comme des petits pains* ('to sell like rolls', identical to the German *wie warme Semmeln weggehen*, and very close to 'to sell like

hot cakes'), *marcher sur des oeufs* ('to walk on eggshells'),
or *c'est pas de la tarte* ('it's not pie' – the negative version
of our 'it's a piece of cake', i.e. something tricky or
difficult). But others are completely unique and, well,
just so quintessentially French: *retombler comme un soufflé*
('to sink like a soufflé' = to fall flat, run out of steam);
mettre la main à la pâte ('to put your hand to the pastry'
= to put your shoulder to the wheel, pitch in); *pédaler
dans la choucroute* ('to pedal in the sauerkraut' = to get
nowhere fast); *chanter comme une casserole* ('to sing like
a saucepan' = to sing appallingly badly).

Take the example of a single, humble vegetable like the
cabbage. Any number of idioms attach to it in French,
including *faire ses choux gras* ('to make one's cabbages
fatty' = to use something to one's own advantage);
ménager la chèvre et le chou ('to deal with the goat and the
cabbage' = to have a foot in both camps); *aller planter ses
choux ailleurs* ('to go and plant one's cabbages elsewhere'
= to seek pastures new); and *être dans les choux* ('to be in
the cabbages' = to bring up the rear).

And whereas we Anglo-Saxons prosaically urge drivers
to get a move on by saying 'Put your foot down!' or
'Step on the gas!', the French equivalent is *Appuyez sur le
champignon!* Who but they would have seen a likeness
between an accelerator pedal and a mushroom?

Chapter 5

MILITARIA

Armed conflict; it's always been with us, and will remain so. Along the way, it has spawned huge numbers of phrases and idioms, many of which we don't even recognise as military-based anymore. Classical warfare gave us the 'Pyrrhic victory', the 18th–19th centuries provided 'biting the bullet', 'meeting one's Waterloo' and 'having a field day', while the First and Second World Wars generated, respectively, 'basket case' and 'gone for a Burton', alongside many others.

Now that war has become a 24-hour rolling news spectator sport (or at least, the edited titbits that liaison officers feed to 'embedded' correspondents), the richest seam of new military terminology is Pentagon Newspeak. We lap up and regurgitate the media-management euphemisms created to make killing people sound less messy, less brutal: 'surgical strike', 'soft target' and 'ethnic cleansing'. And one that has already made the crossover from the operations briefing room to common parlance: 'collateral damage'.

SWIFT-BOATING (US)

The practice of smearing a rival, particularly a political opponent during a campaign

This curious expression derives from the 2004 US presidential campaign when the incumbent George W. Bush, standing for a second term, was opposed by John Kerry, the Democratic Party nominee. Although seen as a rather aloof figure, Kerry had several things in his favour, including the unpopularity of George Bush among large sections of the population and the coincidence of sharing the JFK initials with President John

Kennedy. In addition, Kerry should have enjoyed the respect usually extended in the Unites States to military personnel since he served in Vietnam as commander of a Swiftboat patrol craft. (The name of the boat supposedly derived from the acronym Shallow Water Inshore Fast Tactical Craft.) Kerry had been wounded and decorated, and on his return to the United States joined an anti-war veterans' group and even testified before a Senate committee on atrocities committed by US troops. More than thirty years later, this could be presented by his Republican opponents as unpatriotic behaviour, but the real damage was done by those questioning his war service. An organisation calling itself Swift Boat Veterans for Truth disputed his fitness to command, the severity of his wounds, the validity of the medals he'd received, and generally undermined Kerry's standing as a presidential candidate. The allegations of the Swift Boat Veterans, who were funded in part by wealthy Republican sympathisers, were themselves disputed. This war of claim and counterclaim formed a substantial strand in the 2004 presidential campaign, which Kerry lost, and the term 'swiftboating' entered the language as a synonym for 'smearing' or 'character assassination'. Of course, the accusation that one's opponents are engaging in swiftboat tactics may in itself be a form of smear.

PREPARE YOURSELF FOR ST-QUENTIN
(SPANISH)

Armarse la de San Quintín – **to raise hell/kick up an almighty fuss**

St-Quentin, a French town just south of the border with Belgium, was the site of a bloody clash in 1557, during the Franco–Habsburg War of 1551–59. A heavily outnumbered force from the Spanish Netherlands, with some Dutch and English support, routed the troops of King Henri II of France. It has not only gone down in history as a great feat of Spanish arms, but is also recalled in this idiom for the sheer carnage that occurred there: out of a total of some 24,000 French infantry and cavalry, no fewer than 14,000 were left dead or injured.

The battle also provided the impetus to one of early modern Europe's most spectacular building projects. Touched by the terrible bloodshed his troops had wrought, and to give thanks for the decisive victory, Philip II of Spain, who had come to the throne only the year before, ordered construction of the monastery and royal residence of El Escorial at the foot of the Sierra de Guadarrama, northwest of Madrid. The wider settlement around this huge new edifice was christened San Lorenzo de El Escorial; the feast day of the early Christian martyr St Lawrence of Rome is 10 August, the date on which the terrible battle took place. To further underscore the religious significance of the site, Philip ordered that the building's groundplan should resemble a gridiron, the instrument of torture by which St Lawrence met his death during the persecutions conducted by the Roman emperor Valerian in AD 258.

BUY THE FARM (US)
Die/get killed

There is no doubt about the meaning of 'buy the farm', but equally there is no generally accepted explanation of the origins of a phrase which first emerged in the 1950s. To 'buy it/one' has been slang usage since the First World War to describe death in combat, generally expressed in a past-tense formula such as 'He's bought it'. Buying the farm tended to be associated with a flyer's death, as a result of a crash or enemy action, although it can now apply to any sudden and dramatic end. But where does the farm come in?

One explanation is straightforward and has nothing to do with flying: it is that a farmer's family would own the farm they lived on only when the head of the household died and the life insurance enabled them to pay off the mortgage. Getting possession of the farm was, therefore, equated with death. Other explanations are, variously, more sentimental or cynical. In one the expression derives, via films or perhaps real life, from the wish expressed by an airman to settle down on a farmstead once he retires/the war is over. So, when he comes to a premature end, the wry comment will be made that he's 'bought the farm'.

Other explanations give a literal, monetary meaning to the term. The insurance or compensation paid out on the death of a combatant would have been enough to enable his family to pay off the mortgage on their farm, an explanation made slightly more plausible by the fact that a fair proportion of the Second World War and Korean War pilots would have been single young men from rural communities with parents surviving as their beneficiaries. Alternatively, the money was paid in compensation for damage caused by any USAF crash on the farm itself, after the farmer sued the government. In both accounts the pilot is ironically said to have 'bought the farm' through his own misfortune. The second of these rather limited and tortuous derivations – how many jets, exactly, are required to crash on farm land or buildings to propel an expression into general use? – sounds like after-the-fact reasoning. There was a New Zealand phrase, 'rehab farm', in use after the Second World War, applied to a farm bought with a government loan by members of the returning military, with 'rehab' meaning simply the assisted reintroduction of a soldier into civilian life. In this case, though, 'buying the farm' is literal and positive rather than being a euphemism for death.

The true explanation for 'buy the farm' may never be uncovered. But it is worth noting that one of the old applications of 'farm' was simply to any tract of ground. There is an old idea that the grave is the last bit of land that any of us will possess. Graveyards have plots, like building sites. 'God's little acre' is a folksy US term for a cemetery. Behind the homely 'buy the farm' may lurk the notion of the possession of a final bit of land, a purchase which, as the gravedigger says in *Hamlet*, will last till Doomsday.

ZERO-EIGHT-FIFTEEN (German)

Null-acht-fünfzehn – **bog standard/run of the mill**

Strange to relate, but in the days before international copyright law and licensing agreements, you could just filch someone else's bright idea and get away with it. Especially if you were an unhinged militarist autocrat with scant regard for the niceties of legality. When US inventor Hiram Maxim unveiled the world's first fully automatic machine gun in 1884, its terrifying efficiency saw armies around the world scramble to re-equip themselves. Democracies such as the United States and the United Kingdom played by the rules and paid Maxim his dues, but Imperial Germany and Tsarist Russia simply copied the gun and produced it themselves, as the MG [*Maschinengewehr*] 08 and the *Pulemyot Maxima* PM1910 respectively (the numbers denoting the year of adoption by the countries' armed forces). In Germany's case, by the time the First World

War broke out, the MG 08 had gone through several variants, of which the most widely deployed – notably on the Western Front – was the relatively light and portable MG 08/15. In all, some 130,000 were manufactured.

Like most early machine guns, Germany's *Ersatz* Maxim was water-cooled, belt-fed and cumbersome, and required a team of specially trained troops to fire it. But it was by no means a bad weapon: waves of French *poilus* fell victim to it during the costly Chemin des Dames offensive of April 1917. Yet thanks to its ubiquity and its longevity (when Germany went to war again in 1939, it was still the *Wehrmacht*'s main machine gun), it gradually became a byword among soldiers for anything standard-issue and bog-standard.

Squaddies operate in a world of acronyms and abbreviations that are gibberish to those of us in Civvy Street. Similar jokey coinages originated from the US Army in the same period: SNAFU ('Situation Normal: All Fucked Up') and FUBAR ('Fucked Up Beyond All Recognition'). What enabled '08/15' to cross from military jargon into general usage was a trilogy of popular novels of that title (with the respective subtitles; *In the Barracks, At War*, and *Back Home*) written in the 1950s by Hans Hellmut Kirst, which were later made into very successful films.

So, don't use this phrase unless you mean to damn something with faint praise. At least, not in Germany. On his blog, a frustrated expatriate Anglo-Saxon marooned in Switzerland suggests that '08/15' is a condition that every Swiss aspires to. Echoes here of Harry Lime's immortal speech in *The Third Man*: 'In Italy for 30 years under the Borgias they had warfare, terror, murder and bloodshed, but they produced Michelangelo, Leonardo da Vinci and the Renaissance. In

Switzerland they had brotherly love – they had 500 years of democracy and peace, and what did that produce? The cuckoo clock.'

(NOT) ON MY WATCH (US)

Declaration that certain events will (or will not) be permitted to occur during an officeholder's period of responsibility

Shortly before his uncontested election to a fourth term as FIFA President, Sepp Blatter was asked at a press conference: 'How could you let the reputation of FIFA be so damaged on your watch?' His response was to brandish his wrist-watch. This was apparently Blatter's idea of a joke – a visual pun – rather than a demonstration of his failure to understand a US idiom which has grown increasingly popular on the British side of the Atlantic. 'Watch' has plenty of meanings but the phrase 'on my watch', more often found in the negative 'not on my watch', derives from the nautical practice of dividing the 24-hour day into watches or periods of duty, usually four hours in length. The senior crew member in charge of any given watch would be responsible for the safety of the ship, and so would carry the can if anything went wrong. This explains why the phrase tends to be expressed as a negative, since the person in charge of the ship is looking to avoid trouble and will be relieved if nothing untoward happens. 'Not on my watch' is regularly used in the context of American politics, and comes naturally to US Presidents, who combine being at the top of the political tree with the post of commander-in-chief. After reading an article about genocide in Rwanda, George W. Bush is supposed to have scribbled 'Not on my watch!' in the margin. The phrase has a faintly macho tinge to it and it fits neatly with the concept of the nation state as a great ship navigating its way through the perilous waters of the modern world. When uttered by British politicians or business leaders, '(not) on my watch' does not have quite the same resonance.

MORE WAS LOST IN CUBA (Spanish)

Más se perdió en Cuba – **worse things happen at sea**

This consolatory phrase was first used by Spanish veterans returning from the disastrous conflict between their country and the United States in 1898, which saw Spain lose her last significant overseas territories of Cuba, Puerto Rico and the Philippines. The *Desastre del 98*, the final crumbling of a once-mighty empire, left deep scars on the Spanish psyche.

The US had long signalled its hostility to European intervention in the Americas. The Monroe Doctrine of 1823 enshrined this principle, while at the same time pledging recognition of existing colonies. Yet growing public anger at Spanish suppression of the independence movement on Cuba pushed the two countries inexorably towards war. Hostilities began on 25 April 1898 and ceased on 12 August.

By the first days of July, the land fighting on Cuba had resolved itself into a siege of the major port of Santiago de Cuba. But for the defenders, worse things were indeed about to happen at sea. When, on 3 July, Spain's Caribbean Squadron of armoured cruisers and destroyers attempted to break out of Santiago harbour, it was intercepted by the US Navy. Within an hour, five of the six Spanish ships had either been sunk or forced to run aground, while the final vessel was later scuttled by her crew. This crushing defeat made surrender of the Spanish garrison on the island inevitable.

The Americans lost only one sailor in this action, against 474 Spanish dead or wounded. But two months before the war broke out, on 15 February, the US Navy had suffered its own grievous casualties (274 dead) when the battleship USS *Maine* blew up and sank in Havana harbour. A mine was claimed to be the cause of the explosion, providing newspaper proprietors William Randolph Hearst and Joseph Pulitzer with the *casus belli* they had long been agitating for. If the brief Spanish-American War is recalled in the Spanish language through *Más se perdió…* , then the most memorable phrase it spawned in English was the battlecry of the American yellow press; 'Remember the *Maine*! To hell with Spain!' A 1976 inquiry headed by US Admiral Hyman G. Rickover determined that the *Maine* was destroyed by an internal explosion, probably triggered by a fire in a coal bunker igniting the battleship's forward magazine. Of course, in our more enlightened times, it's inconceivable that a country might go to war for entirely fanciful reasons. Isn't it?

GONE FOR A BURTON (UK)
Lost/destroyed

This is one of those expressions whose origins are completely obscure (like 'the full Monty' or the 'whole nine yards') and so provide a field day for lexicographers and idiom-book compilers. Its earliest uses during the 1940s relate to aircraft crashes so it can fairly confidently be stated that 'gone for a Burton' is a piece of RAF slang. The capitalisation of Burton, as in 'He went for a Burton over France last year', suggests one of three sources: the Staffordshire town of Burton-on-Trent, which was and is a brewing centre, or a type of ale named after the town or the firm of tailors founded by Montague Burton before the First World War. If it is the town itself rather than the beer which is the source, then the only explanation would seem to be that Burton-on-Trent is rhyming slang for 'went' or, in full, 'went west'. To 'go west' has long been a slightly euphemistic term for to 'die' (probably because the sun sets in the west and possibly because of an association with the old Celtic tradition that the west is the abode of the dead). But the expression generally appears in the form of 'he's gone west' rather than 'he went west', which casts doubt on the rhyming-slang notion.

A more plausible explanation relates the phrase to a supposed series of pre-1939 advertisements promoting a Burton's ale, each featuring an empty space in a line-up of, say, musical players and bearing the words 'gone for a Burton'. It sounds like a good concept for a campaign. Sadly, there is no evidence that any such advertisements existed (and, even if they did, it is just as likely that any slogan would have read 'gone for a Burton's'). The link with the tailors Montague Burton is two-fold. One suggests that during the Second World War the RAF used billiard halls, often sited above Burton's shops, as medical centres or places for testing Morse code skills. Such an interpretation of 'going for a Burton' would imply failing some examination, whether medical or practical, but this hardly equates to the slang but irreversible sense of the phrase (i.e. dying). Moving downstairs from the billiard hall above the shop, we reach Montague Burton, a company famous for their suits as well as military uniforms. Many individuals must have purchased the suits they wore for funerals at Montague Burton, but going to a funeral is not the same as being dead and buried. In a metaphorical sense, the person who's 'gone for a Burton' could be said to be clothed in a shroud or a 'wooden overcoat' (coffin) but, once again, the derivation is stretched almost to breaking point. Michael Quinion, who is the doyen of word researchers, suggests that the Burton-on-Trent beer connection is the most likely one, despite the lack of hard evidence. The drink link may be reinforced by the fact that RAF wartime slang for the sea was 'drink', and that numbers of pilots were lost when their planes crashed or when they bailed out offshore in the Battle of Britain and later.

THE PRUSSIANS DON'T SHOOT THAT FAST
(GERMAN)

So schnell schießen die Preußen nicht) – **Hold your horses!**

Prussia was a state built on martial might. Its second king, Friedrich Wilhelm I (r.1713–40), turned a modest body of badly equipped and ill-trained troops into a fearsome, 80,000 strong fighting machine – in the process earning himself the soubriquet *Der Soldatenkönig* ('the Soldier King'). Thereafter, this latter-day Sparta carried all before it. Blücher saved Wellington's bacon at Waterloo, while the Austrians were swept aside in a mere seven weeks over the summer of 1866 in the struggle for supremacy among the German-speaking nations. Prussia's ultimate feat of arms came in 1870–71, with the annihilation of Napoleon III's France and proclamation of the German Second Empire in the Hall of Mirrors at Versailles.

Three competing explanations attach to this idiom, each relating to a different aspect of Prussian militarism. The first dates from around 1742, shortly after the accession of the Soldier King's son, Friedrich II (Frederick the Great). Frederick ordered cast into the cannon manufactured for his armies the legend *Ultima ratio regis* ('the king's final argument', an adaptation of the inscription on earlier Spanish artillery pieces, *Ultima ratio regum* – 'the final argument of kings' (pl.)). Thus making the phrase a bit of Prussian propaganda, suggesting that it only went to war as a last resort. This was certainly the meaning Chancellor Otto von Bismarck intended when he used it in 1875 in response to an English journalist who had suggested that Germany might be spoiling for another fight with France.

The second explanation alludes to the Prussian army's practice – at variance with other armies of the period, and long thereafter – of not summarily putting deserters in front of a firing squad. This had nothing to do with humanitarianism, and everything to do with thrift (supposedly a typical Prussian trait) and lack of resources: the state wasn't so populous that recruits, once having been intensively drilled, could be regarded as expendable if they deserted. So, these poor unfortunates (mostly drafted against their will) were thrashed to within an inch of their lives and returned to the ranks.

The third explanation concerns a weapon that gave the Prussian army a clear advantage over its rivals from the mid-19th century onwards. The Dreyse needle gun, named after its inventor, the Rhineland gunsmith Johann Nikolaus von Dreyse, became the standard Prussian infantry rifle after 1848. Its breech-loading mechanism, in which a needle-like firing pin punctured a paper cartridge, made it far faster to reload than traditional muzzle-loaded muskets. With its rapid rate of fire, the gun played a decisive role in the Battle of Königgrätz (Sadowa), fought in Bohemia on 3 July 1866. The casualty figures speak for themselves: 5,735 Austrian dead compared to

1,900 Prussians. Some authorities believe this bloody engagement gave the idiom its common currency. In this context, the implication is that an over-hasty person is outstripping even the Prussians' impressive speed on the trigger.

SCUTTLEBUTT (US)
Gossip/speculation

Scuttlebutt is a piece of US nautical slang which long ago entered the American mainstream and which is occasionally found in British English, although here it may be explained – and so made more or less redundant – by appearing alongside synonyms such as like 'gossip' or 'rumour'.

A scuttle is a square hole on board ship used for light, ventilation and so on (and, when below the waterline, for scuttling or sinking the vessel). So a scuttled – or holed – butt is the sea-going term for a cask from which water can be drawn. The cask was later replaced by a drinking fountain but the original expression persisted. Since sailors naturally stopped and chatted while they drew water, their gossip took its nickname from the spot where they were standing. Scuttlebutt in the metaphorical sense of 'gossip' is found as early as 1901 but it is likely that the secretive operational conditions of the Second World War particularly encouraged the use of the term in the US Navy. If no one except the senior officers knew where they were going or what they were going to do when they got there, then rumours would have flowed even more freely round the drinking fountain, as shown by this 1943 quotation from the *Baltimore Sun*: 'Also a cause for betting was the ultimate destination. In navy slang "scuttlebutt" was rife and had the ship bound anywhere from China to Murmansk.'

So the scuttlebutt as an object is the nautical equivalent of the office water cooler, a magnet for brief bouts of off-duty socialising. It ought to be noted, though, that the metaphorical scuttlebutt is relatively informed rather than being wild rumour or unfounded gossip. It is practised by insiders. The trouble is that they are not quite inside enough. (See also **Furphy**)

ZAMORA WASN'T TAKEN IN AN HOUR
(SPANISH)

No se ganó Zamora en una hora – **Rome wasn't built in a day**

The strategic city of Zamora in Castile and León, on the Duero River near the border with Portugal, was renowned for being a tough nut to crack and has gone down in Spanish idiomatic usage as an exhortation to persevere.

The phrase derives from not one, but two sieges of the town, some 400 years apart. Both were the result of internecine feuding over succession to the Castilian throne. By 1072, Sancho II, one of three sons of King Ferdinand I, had defeated his brothers in the struggle to succeed their father; the only place to still resist was Zamora, which had been bequeathed to his sister Doña Urraca. While Sancho was besieging the city, a nobleman from within posing as a defector lured him into a private meeting and assassinated him. The second siege took place in 1476, during the War of the Castilian Succession between supporters of Isabella of Castile and her niece Juana la Beltraneja. Juana was Portuguese Queen Consort and was promised in marriage to her maternal uncle, King Afonso V of Portugal. When his forces crossed the border and surrounded Zamora in February 1476, however, a combination of resilient defence and a harsh winter exacted a greater toll on the besiegers than the besieged, and the Portuguese ruler was subsequently defeated at the nearby Battle of Toro.

Note that neither action was successful. A curious image, therefore, to hold up as an illustration of the virtues of patient persistence.

CATCH-22 (US)

A no-win situation

The title of the most famous and, arguably, the best antiwar novel of all time has entered the language to describe a situation in which success or any kind of happy outcome is impossible or, more broadly, refers to the necessity to choose between courses of action all of which have poor consequences. There is a Kafkaesque whiff to Catch-22 since it is usually human rules, bureaucracy or sheer stupidity which cause its victim to feel persecuted and helpless.

The phrase originated with Joseph Heller's novel, published in 1961 and set on a Mediterranean island in the latter stages of the Second World War. The central character, an airman called Yossarian, is determined to survive or escape the war but his efforts are frustrated by the crazy logic of higher command, particularly in constantly upping the number of bombing missions. One way out would be to plead insanity. But there's a catch. In Joseph Heller's own words:

'There was only one catch and that was Catch-22, which specified that a concern for one's safety in the face of dangers that were real and immediate was the process of a rational mind. Orr [a pilot] was crazy and could be grounded. All he had to do was ask; and as soon as he did, he would no longer be crazy and would have to fly more

missions. Orr would be crazy to fly more missions and
sane if he didn't, but if he was sane he had to fly them. If
he flew them he was crazy and didn't have to; but if he
didn't want to he was sane and had to.'

Heller was a slow, methodical writer, beginning *Catch-22*
while working as an advertising copywriter in New York in
1953. The work-in-progress first saw the light of day in a
literary quarterly in 1955 under the title *Catch-18*. And so it
might have stayed had not another novel using the same
number appeared just as Heller's book was being prepared for
publication. *Mila 18*, by the one-time best-selling but now
almost forgotten Leon Uris, took its title from a Warsaw street
number where the Jewish resistance held out against the Nazis
in 1942. So the number in Heller's title was changed from 18
to 22 to avoid confusion with Uris's. It's hard not to conclude
that the enforced change of number/title was to the ultimate
benefit of *Catch-22*, perhaps contributing significantly to its
global success. *Catch-22* has more of a ring to it than *Catch-18*,
and the novel's trapped logic is better reflected in the repeated
digits of 22.

ONLY UNDERSTAND 'STATION' (German)

Immer nur Bahnhof verstehen – **to not understand a thing/
fail to catch something**

The railways played a key role in the First World War.
In August 1914, Germany's Schlieffen Plan, the strategy of
delivering a knockout blow to France in the west before
redeploying troops east to overwhelm the Russians, was
predicated on mass mobilisation of men and equipment by
train.

In 1918, as German morale collapsed in the face of the United States' entry into the war the effective Allied strategy of 'creeping barrages', and shortages and starvation began to set in on the home front, soldiers deserted en masse. This idiom is reckoned to come from this period, when large detachments of troops, desperate to make it back to their families, seemed oblivious to everything but news of their demobilisation and transport home by train.

Nowadays, the phrase has taken on the extended meaning of not hearing something properly or catching only snatches of it. This probably has to do with the general hubbub that often characterises busy stations, intermittently drowning out public-address announcements about arrivals and departures.

HOIST WITH ONE'S OWN PETARD (UK)
To be caught in a trap of one's own making

This is a familiar phrase but the 'hoist' part of it sometimes misleads people into the idea that a petard must be some kind of flagpole. Far from it. The first dictionary citation for the expression is from *Hamlet* so it is probable that Shakespeare was the creator of it. The words occur in the play when Hamlet is about to be sent from Denmark to England, escorted by Rosencrantz and Guildenstern. He expects to be betrayed by these old friends but believes he can outmanouevre them with his own cunning:

> '*Let it work;*
> *For 'tis the sport to have the enginer*
> *Hoist with his own petar.*'

In the event, Hamlet substitutes their names for his own on the death warrant which they are carrying.

A 'petard' (or 'petar') was an explosive device used commonly in siege work. A primitive mine or bomb, it was placed against an enemy gate or wall to which it might have been conveyed via a trench or tunnel. The engineer, Shakespeare's 'enginer', could be the soldier who dug the excavation as well as the one who planted the bomb (The Royal Engineers were formerly Royal Sappers and Miners). A misjudged length of fuse or other accident might result in the deliverer of the bomb being blown up by his own weapon. There was an element of subterfuge in the activities of the 'enginer', as suggested by Hamlet's use of the phrase, and this survives in the current application of the phrase. It is close in meaning to being too clever or cunning for one's own good.

GROUND ZERO (US)

The point on the surface of the earth at or closest to a nuclear explosion; a place or time which marks the beginning of something absolutely new

'Ground zero' was the original designation for the place closest to a nuclear blast and was used in reports on the effects of the bombs dropped on Hiroshima and Nagasaki towards the end of the Second World War. Even before that, it applied to the area around the tower holding the first atomic bomb detonated experimentally at the White Sands Proving Ground in New Mexico in July 1945, three weeks before the first bomb was used against Japan. The clinical objectivity of the phrase indicates its military/scientific origin. Although it retained its nuclear associations – horrific if pondered closely – 'ground zero' could also be used about a variety of non-nuclear, non-disastrous starting-points as in these references from the *Guardian* to Islington ('Ground Zero in the [Tony] Blair revolution') or Greenwich ('the millennium's ground zero'). Indeed, the phrase was often so diluted by general use that it meant not much more than 'square one', as in 'We're starting at ground zero'. Then came the terrorist attacks of 9/11 and the aerial destruction of the World Trade Center. The suddenness and traumatic effect made for more a more justified use of the expression and straightaway the term was being employed in this context ('"ground zero," as it was being called by hospital workers and police officers, was Lower Manhattan': *New York Times*, 12 September 2001). When referring to the site, the phrase is often capitalised and there is now a Ground Zero Museum.

BITE THE BULLET (UK/US?)

To be stoical when undergoing a painful experience; to accept an unpleasant truth

This is one of those expressions which has contentious origins even if there is general agreement that it must have a military connection. There are two popular derivations. One dates from the time of the Indian Mutiny (1857), an uprising against British rule in the subcontinent which was provoked, in part, by the command that the sepoys or Indian soldiers should literally bite the bullet. This procedure was necessary because, to load the new Enfield rifles with which they had been issued, the sepoys had to bite off the end of each paper cartridge to release the gunpowder inside. It was believed that the grease used to lubricate and seal the cartridges was made from animal fat, consumption of which is forbidden to Muslims (if pork fat) and Hindus (if beef). Rumours spread that this was not some accidental oversight on the part of the British and the East India Company but a deliberate insult to the indigenous religions. So the order to 'bite the bullet' was one of the sparks that fired a period of rebellion and savage repression.

One of the problems with the Indian Mutiny theory is that the meaning of the phrase works against what the sepoys actually did. Arguably, by *refusing* to bite the bullet they brought down much more trouble on their heads than if they had obeyed the order. Of course, the expression could apply to soldiers other than sepoys, to those who would have no religious objection to 'biting the bullet' before loading their rifles. If this is the prelude to military action, something which has to be endured and which cannot be avoided, then 'biting the bullet' becomes part of the run-up to battle, and the undertones of stoicism and inevitability in the phrase make better sense.

Another popular explanation is that it derives from the practice, in the days before anaesthetics, of having wounded soldiers bite on a bullet during an operation so as to prevent them biting through their tongues or crying out and distracting the surgeon. It has been observed that the survival chances of a soldier about to undergo an amputation would not have been enhanced if he were required to hold between his teeth a smallish object while lying on his back and in an agonised state. Either the traditional strip of leather or even a length of wood, both items which could not be easily swallowed, seems to be a better bet. Yet there is a link between biting the bullet and a tormenting experience. An early 19th century dictionary of slang and colloquialisms provided an explanation of how some soldiers stopped themselves crying out, or becoming 'nightingales', when they were being flogged with the cat-o'-nine tails for a breach of discipline. This silence, says Francis Grose, the dictionary compiler, 'is a point of honour in some regiments, among the grenadiers' and to maintain it during their torment 'they chew a bullet'. This may be the origin of the slightly different 'bite the bullet' but, if so, the earlier expression almost certainly became conflated with the action of biting off the end of a cartridge to load a rifle.

SON OF A GUN (US/UK)

A rascal; an exclamation indicating surprise or irritation

There is a fairly literal explanation of this phrase, which goes back to the early 18th century. A 'son of a gun' was a child born to a woman on board a naval vessel. The gun allusion is explained either by the baby's having been born behind makeshift screens spread between a couple of the cannon, or to the entry in the ship's log which did not (or could not) specify the child's paternity and so simply referred to him as a 'son of the gun'. A mid-Victorian dictionary of naval terms explains that it was a slightly contemptuous term while an earlier compendium of slang, published in the more liberal days before the accession of Queen Victoria, bluntly defines the expression as 'a soldier's bastard'. It is quite likely that the term originates with this basic sense, and that the naval link comes later. The phallic associations of the gun reinforce the image of the randy, carefree soldier.

Alternatively, the expression may be a watered-down version of the much older insult 'son of a bitch'. On this reading, 'gun' is employed for its monosyllabic rhyme with 'son', and the parental emphasis is transferred from the female to the male. In the Unites States, both phrases may be used to describe individuals, although 'son of a bitch' (often appearing in contracted forms like sonofabitch or s.o.b.) is almost always a term of abuse while the euphemistic 'son of a gun' conveys a note of approval, even admiration. This 'son of a gun' may be a bit of a lad but he's also a regular guy. Both phrases also serve as general exclamations of shock or surprise. The 'bitch' version is still described as vulgar while the 'gun' is perfectly acceptable as a colloquialism.

DRAW A LINE IN THE SAND (US)
To mark a boundary/impose a limit

The metaphorical act of 'drawing a line in the sand' is a development of the older expression 'draw the line', indicating a division between different things, and perhaps deriving from the boundaries of ploughed land or from the in-out lines required in a ball game. The refinement involving sand surely arises from the fact that sand is easy to draw in, and is illustrated by two apocryphal stories. In 168 BC, during an invasion of Egypt by Antiochus, the king of a regional power[1], the Roman consul drew a line in the sand round the monarch and told him he could not step outside the circle until he agreed to withdraw his forces. In another time and continent, during the siege of the Alamo by Mexican forces in 1836, the Texan colonel in command of the mission station is supposed to have gathered his men together and, after telling them that defeat was almost inevitable, drew a line in the sand (or dirt) with his sword and announced that those who were willing to die for freedom should cross the line and join him. All but one of the soldiers did so. Each story carries a slightly different sense of the metaphor: the Roman tale imposes a limit ('this far and no

---

1 Antiochus was king of the Seleucids, a Syrian dynasty. They invaded Egypt when it was under the Ptolomies but regarded it as part of Rome's sphere of influence.

further') while the Texan legend has more to do with other figurative expressions like 'crossing the Rubicon', since to step over this line in the sand is to pass the point of no return.

The expression was given new currency after the Iraqi invasion of Kuwait in 1990 by (the first) President Bush's announcement that 'a line has been drawn in the sand'. Bush's use, which was an ultimatum to Iraqi dictator Saddam Hussein, was more like the Roman consul's threat than the Texan colonel's invitation. The continued involvement of the United States and other countries in wars in the Arabian desert has ensured that sand remains part of the 'draw a line' formula. (see also **Cross the Rubicon**)

ON THE GRAPEVINE (US)

Relating to news, rumour or gossip passed on unofficially

This expression emerged in the United States not long after the establishment of the telegraph as the quickest and most up-to-date means of communication in the middle of the 19th century. Presumably, the 'on the grapevine' metaphor is drawn from the similarity between the lengths of telegraph wire stretching in all directions across the country and the creepers and tendrils of the vine. Indeed, the parallel between the man-made wire and the natural one is made explicit in a report filed by a newspaper correspondent in Nashville, Tennessee, in 1862 during the early stages of the Civil War: 'Last night I telegraphed you that the rebels had evacuated Murfreesboro and retired to Tallahoma. Today the grapevine says that the rebels at Murfreesboro have been strongly reinforced and that they are going to attack us.'

Information heard 'on the grapevine' may be less reliable than the news passed on via the telegraph system but it has a human, gossipy dimension which is missing from the official version. Curiously, the use now of media such as Twitter brings together gossip and technology in a way unprecedented in history. The grapevine has turned electronic. A related phrase, though now out of use, is 'the clothesline telegraph'. This was used on at least one occasion during the American Civil War when the Union and Confederate forces were encamped on opposite banks of a river. A woman working as a laundress at the headquarters of a Confederate general positioned the washing on the line according to the movements of the various rebel commanders. Her husband, on the other shore, was able to interpret the messages and pass information to the Union forces.

FIFTH COLUMN (US/UK; ORIGINALLY SPANISH)

A treacherous group inside a government, organisation etc., which is secretly dedicated to its subversion or overthrow

It is rare to be able to locate an expression so precisely as it is with 'fifth column'. Soon after the start of the Spanish Civil War (1936–39), Emilio Mola, a rebel general, was asked by a reporter which of four converging columns of troops would capture Madrid, one of the cities in the hands of the Republican (i.e. anti-Fascist) forces. The reply was that Madrid would fall to 'the fifth' column, a piece of propaganda implying that there were enough sympathisers of the rebel cause to rise up within the city when the moment came. Not long afterwards, Mola died in a plane crash while the city which he threatened was not to fall until the end of the Civil War. But his expression – in Spanish, *una quinta columna* – evidently answered a political/lingustic need, for it immediately took root in the English language. Ernest

Hemingway, acting as a war correspondent and with Republican loyalties, took it for the title of his only play, *The Fifth Column*, which was staged in 1937 in Madrid while the city was under siege.

Fears about Nazi spies and would-be collaborators made the 'fifth column' a natural phrase for Winston Churchill to employ in the early stages of the Second World War. Churchill also applied the term to the operation of the Communist parties in the West after the end of the war. President Roosevelt went one stage further by referring to a 'sixth column'. Roosevelt's remarks, which seem to have been directed mostly at reporters, described those who spread propaganda through their writings along with 'rumor, cocktail parties and tea fights'. The expression is still going strong, particularly in politics and warfare, so that any group suspected of having a subversive influence may be termed a 'fifth column'. A fifth columnist is distinct from a 'fellow traveller', who is a sympathiser with a political cause (historically, with Communism) but not someone actively working for that cause.

CUT AND RUN (US?)
To leave quickly

Like so many idioms, 'cut and run' has a nautical source (but see **All at Sea?** on page 101), although there is some dispute over the original context of the phrase. It might derive from the way a ship effected a quick getaway in an emergency when, instead of weighing anchor, the sailors would slice through the hemp cable and permit the vessel to run before the wind. This would be a panic-stricken measure, not least because of the loss of an anchor. Another explanation holds that ships are not capable of such sudden acceleration and that, regardless of circumstances, there must always be time to haul the anchor aboard. This more positive sense of 'cut and run' refers to the practice of keeping sails lightly furled with ropes so that a few quick slashes would release them, perhaps before making a surprise attack.

The earliest (18th century) references are literal and 'cut and run' does not seem to have turned into a metaphor until the middle of the 19th century. The phrase could be used at first in a neutral sense to mean simply 'depart rapidly' rather than 'run away'. Now it is now almost always pejorative, and implies a shirking of responsibility, even cowardice. This may be partly to do with its frequent appearance in a military context. The political columnist and wordsmith William Safire notes that 'cut and run' has been used in connection with US involvement in foreign countries since at least the Second World War. It acquired renewed prominence during the war in Iraq when President George W. Bush declared that the United States would not follow a 'cut and run' policy. The phrase became a near equivalent for 'rout' or 'defeat' and so, as intended, put any opponent of withdrawal from Iraq on the back foot.

BASKET CASE (US)

An individual, institution or country that is so badly damaged as to be incapable of functioning

Originally (and grimly) applying to a soldier who lost all four limbs in wartime and could only have been carried about in a hamper-like 'basket', this expression has acquired a sense which is entirely figurative. Its earliest appearance is just after the First World War but only in the form of a denial from the Surgeon-General of the US Army to the effect that there was 'any foundation for the stories that have been circulating of the existence of basket cases in our hospitals.' Towards the end of the Second World War, a similar denial was issued by the authorities. Whatever the rumours, it was asserted that there were no cases of men hospitalised with both arms and legs amputated. Despite this, *Time* magazine claimed to have tracked down two such individuals. The expression is now used most often in relation to economic failure, so that a country which is in such dire financial straits that it is entirely dependent on outside help is routinely referred to as a 'basket case'.

ALL AT SEA?

Little wonder that Britain's long history of seafaring should have given rise to a whole slew of nautical idioms. But it has become a cliché to attribute every last phrase to this proud tradition, so much so that etymologists have jokingly posited the existence of a shadowy pressure group: CANOE ('Committee for Ascribing a Naval Origin to Everything'). It seems that even some of our more august institutions, which should know better, have fallen victim. For instance, at its various sites, the Imperial War Museum has boards presenting the 'Top 5 Naval Phrases', including: *Getting Your Own Back – If the wind was blowing in the wrong direction when using the toilets (or 'heads') on a ship you would 'get your own back'.* But this surely can't be right: to get your own back involves exacting satisfying revenge, not scoring an own goal.

Of course, there are plenty of idioms whose nautical provenance is clear and indisputable: batten down the hatches; shipshape and Bristol fashion; to give someone a wide berth; or, indeed, all at sea. And then there are others that don't immediately reveal their origin but which nevertheless definitely come from this world:

- **Slush fund** – from the perk granted to ships' cooks, of skimming off and saving pork and beef fat ('slush') for sale when they put ashore. The proceeds were shared among the crew.

- **In the offing** – the 'offing' denoted the area of sea visible from dry land. A ship arriving and expected to dock with the next high tide was therefore 'in the offing'.

- **Hard and fast** – originally describing a firmly beached ship or boat.

- **Taken aback** – if a ship turned unexpectedly into the wind so that its sails were blown flat against the masts and spars holding them, it was said to be 'taken aback'.

So, if someone comes to you peddling a sailor's yarn about the naval roots of a common phrase, *caveat emptor.*

Chapter 6

THE DAILY GRIND

'The trivial round, the common task/Would furnish all we ought to ask...', runs a 19th-century hymn. The Christian work ethic in a nutshell: whatever our station in life, we should carry out our allotted duties with a glad heart, our eyes firmly fixed on the prize of a reward in Heaven for a life well-lived in this Vale of Tears. Work was deemed to have an ennobling effect, giving people dignity and a sense of purpose. The alternative was a sinful, restless hankering after a life of ease here below, wallowing in undeserved material luxury (see **A Fool's Paradise** in Chapter 13).

As Christianity's influence waned, this praise of dutiful diligence was drowned out by more cynical voices. Jerome K. Jerome, in *Three Men in a Boat* (1889), famously observed: 'I like work; it fascinates me. I could sit and watch it for hours.' Later, in swinging, carefree, employment-rich 1968, a comedy film told us that *Work is a Four-letter Word*. But for all his posturing as an idler, Jerome was really a self-made man who clawed his way up through sheer hard graft from humble beginnings to become a hugely successful author: *Three Men in a Boat* sold over a million copies in its first 20 years of publication.

However much we may hate the dreary routine of work, we don't half miss it if it evaporates into the living hell of unemployment. This ambivalent attitude to how we earn our daily crust resonates in some of the work-related idioms we have collected here.

SUBWAY, WORK, SLEEP (FRENCH)
Métro, boulot, dodo – **The daily grind/the same old same old**

This succinct figure of speech has more than a hint of Gallic existential *ennui* about it, and captures well the relentless tedium of the daily urban round of commuting, office drudgery and hitting the sack. The first element is self-explanatory, while *boulot* is a slang term for work and *dodo* a childish word for sleep ('beddy-byes'). The rhymed endings of the three juxtaposed two-syllable words only serve to underscore the stultifying, inescapable monotony of it all.

It is the creation of the Romanian-born naturalised French writer Pierre Béarn (1902–2004), being an abbreviation of the last line of his 1951 poem *Couleurs d'usine* ('Factory colours'). The final stanza is worth quoting in full:

Au déboule garçon pointe ton numéro
Pour gagner ainsi le salaire
D'une morne jour utilitaire
Métro, boulot, bistro, mégots, dodo, zero

['Rush in, boy, punch your number
To earn your salary
For another dreary workaday day
Subway, work, bars, fags, sleep, nothing']

The phrase entered popular consciousness during the upheavals in Paris in 1968, when a general strike and rioting came close to bringing about the collapse of the ageing Charles de Gaulle's government. Students used it to encourage disgruntled workers at Renault's huge Boulogne-Billancourt car assembly plant in the western suburbs to add their industrial muscle to the protest. Sprayed on walls around the French capital, the slogan proclaimed a fundamental rejection of the bourgeois rat race.

In the event, order was restored, the Fifth Republic survived, and the phrase turned from a revolutionary clarion call of the *soixante-huitards* into a resigned lament of weary wage-slaves.

GOING POSTAL (US)
Flying into a destructive rage, particularly in the workplace

Aficionados of early Robert Redford films may remember the scenes in the conspiracy thriller *Three Days of the Condor* (1975) in which a hit man disguised as a US mailman guns down an office full of covert CIA workers and later tries to shoot Redford, using the same uniform as cover. In August 1986, in a suburb of Oklahoma City, a genuine postman who was about to be sacked for poor performance drew two pistols from his satchel and shot dead fourteen of his fellow workers inside the local post office before committing suicide. In the next 20 years, there were nearly 50 more deaths in shooting incidents involving post-office workers. Some of the violence was attributed to the stresses of the job, ranging from bad weather to foul-tempered customers and bullying management. The term 'going postal' was soon established as a way of describing the rage which could result from workplace frustrations. It even travelled across the Atlantic and provided the title for a Discworld novel by Terry Pratchett. Unhappy with the damage to its image, the US Postal Service commissioned a survey which revealed that job-related deaths and violence were actually lower in the postal service than in other workplaces. Nevertheless, it will be hard to dispose of 'going postal' as a metaphor for a rage which is out of control, especially in the workplace. Equivalents are 'going ballistic' and 'going ape/apeshit'.

FREE LUNCH (US)
Something for nothing

This phrase almost always appears in its negative version as 'there's no such thing as a free lunch' or – in an aggressively demotic form – 'there ain't no such thing as a free lunch'. The closest thing to a literally free lunch was the practice in American saloons and hotels during the 19th century of offering a meal for nothing to patrons as long as they purchased a drink. This was observed by Rudyard Kipling, who had an American wife and lived in the United States for a time. He wrote:

> 'By instinct I sought refreshment, and came upon a barroom full of bad Salon pictures in which men with hats on the backs of their heads were wolfing food from a counter. It was the institution of the "free lunch" I had struck. You paid for a drink and got as much as you wanted to eat. For something less than a rupee a day a man can feed himself sumptuously in San Francisco, even though he be a bankrupt. Remember this if ever you are stranded in these parts.'

These words were published in 1891 but the 'free lunch' custom dates back to the 1840s. It supposedly moved from the west coast to the east, and lasted well into the 20th century.

It soon spawned its opposite – 'there is no free lunch' – to signify that nothing truly comes without a cost. This negative form is particularly popular with right-wing pundits and among free-marketeers since it is a folksy reminder that all those government benefits and grants and handouts which are seemingly delivered without strings have to be paid for by someone. The anti-free-lunch brigade received a boost in 1975 from the publication by economics guru Milton Friedman of a book of essays entitled *There's No Such Thing as a Free Lunch*, at the same time as his ideas were influencing the future administrations of, among others, Margaret Thatcher and Ronald Reagan. For a good while, the expression was used only as a metaphor but it returned to its roots after the 2006 US congressional elections, when there was widespread anger at the way lobbyists were influencing politicians with lavish and literal free lunches. Among the regulations banning the entertainment of elected officials was the so-called 'toothpick rule' which stipulated that nothing more than hors d'oeuvres could be served and that they had to be eaten while standing up. Truly, there is no such thing as a free lunch.

PUT THE KIBOSH ON (US?)
To bring an end to/ruin

Part of most people's daily experience is the sense that things aren't working out quite to plan or, if events go really pear-shaped, a feeling that the kibosh has been put on them. Kibosh? Whether because of its sound, particularly that initial 'k', or because of its slightly wry sense or for both of these reasons, many people have assumed that 'kibosh' *must* be Yiddish. Yet in his dictionary, *The Joys of Yiddish* (first published 1968), Leo Rosten spends three pages on it only to conclude, with humorous exasperation, that it may well not be from that language at all. Although now almost always appearing in the form 'to put the kibosh on', in 19th century slang 'kibosh' by itself meant rubbish, nonsense. Confusingly, 'bosh', a familiar and vigorous term for nonsense, comes from a Turkish expression meaning empty, worthless. It is possible that the 'ki-' prefix is an intensifier, signifying absolute rubbish, yet this does not quite lead to the prevailing sense of 'kibosh' now. Nor are things made any clearer by noting that this puzzling word was also a piece of Victorian slang for 1/6 (or eighteen pence) even if it has been claimed that someone offering such a sum in a small-time auction would put the kibosh on it, i.e. bring the bidding to an end. The most eccentric theory gives the term a Gaelic twist by making it a version of *cie bais* meaning 'cap of death', the cap which a judge donned before pronouncing the death sentence, something which would certainly ruin the defendant's day.

It's clear, then, that no one has much of a notion where 'kibosh' sprang from. But any expression which is widely used, as this one is, answers a need. One reason is surely to do with the satisfying sound which it makes, with the rise of the first 'ki-' syllable and then the crashing down to the earth with the '-bosh'. A related phrase, in British English, is 'put the mockers on', which means not to deride but to put a jinx or curse on something or someone. Unlike 'kibosh', a Yiddish link is more plausible with the 'mockers' (*makes* = plagues).

ABOVE MY PAY GRADE (US)
Beyond my capacity or competency/not my responsibility

'Above my pay grade' originated with the US Marine Corps but has recently spread to other areas of life, from business to politics. The expression is essentially a brush-off, the non-cooperative answer to a request for information or a demand for action. According to a glossary of terms in the Marines' own magazine, *Leatherneck*, it translates as: 'Don't ask me; it is beyond what I'm paid to know.' It is not surprising that such a hierarchical phrase, with its hint of brusqueness, should come from service life. It is also a useful expression in that it combines ignorance or a refusal to help with a dash of don't-blame-me humility. Although generally negative, the verbal equivalent of a shrug of the shoulders or a head-shake, 'above my pay grade' can also be used to indicate arriving at a higher level of attainment. It may occur in contexts as various as a better than expected car interior – or a better than deserved marriage.

The phrase earned some notoriety in August 2008 when Barack Obama, during the US presidential campaign, was asked on television to define the point at which life began, a question which is always fraught for American politicians since the answer reveals something about the candidate's attitude to abortion. Obama replied 'that whether you're looking at it from a theological perspective or a scientific perspective, answering that question with specificity, you know, is above my pay grade'. The answer, modest or evasive depending on the listener's point of view, caused a storm among anti-abortion groups. Obama seemed to realise that it was damaging when a few weeks later he described his use of the expression as being 'too flip'. The converse, 'below one's pay grade', is seen occasionally in the sense of 'inappropriate' or even 'undignified'.

ON THE FRITZ (US)
Broken down/out of order

'On the fritz' can have a slang sense of 'drunk' but its usual US application is to a piece of machinery or gadget which has broken down. As a shortened form of 'Friedrich', Fritz became a popular and mildly abusive term for a German soldier during the First World War, but there seems little reason why this standard colloquialism should have shifted to a car that won't start or a defunct piece of machinery, and in any case the first references occur before the outbreak of war in 1914. A pleasing suggestion is that 'on the fritz' comes from an onomatopoeic rendering of the fizzing sound made by the wiring in machinery as it goes wrong. But both dates and inherent implausibility argue against this. The first citation, from 1903, in the *Oxford English Dictionary* capitalises the word ('They gave an open air [performance] that put our opera house show on the Fritz') and this does point to a person, whether real or fictional, or to a national group, which can hardly be anything other than German. The undeniably German *kaput* or *kaputt* is found in English around the same time, also with the sense of broken but applicable to people as well as machines. *Kaput* is a stronger term, though, and implies a state beyond repair.

NITTY-GRITTY (US)
The fundamentals/the basic questions

There is a story that the term 'nitty-gritty' was coined to describe the debris and waste left in the hold of a slave ship after the unfortunate survivors had been taken off at the end of the journey. This etymology, almost certainly false, was nevertheless in wide enough circulation to get a UK Home Office minister into trouble in 2002 when he talked of getting down to the 'nitty-gritty' during a police conference. An officer complained that if he were to use such language, he would be disciplined. Since any objection to the term seemed absurd, the fuss over 'nitty-gritty' suited the opponents of political correctness.

The term is African-American but it does not appear in print before the early 1940s (further proof that it has nothing to do with the slave trade), when a US newspaper described how a boxer 'steps into the ring in his pretty satin trunks and whips another guy down in the "nitty-gritty"'. Grit may apply to any rocky substance which is ground down into particles. Metaphorically, it stands for toughness and irreducibility. So, there is probably the implication behind 'nitty gritty' that, once you have got to that level, you cannot go any further (just as the boxer who is knocked down cannot go further than the floor). The phrase also hints at the difficult, perhaps intractable, details of a question. And what about the 'nitty' bit? It has been suggested that this comes from the nit, the head louse or its egg, and so by extension is a reference to things which are both small and unpleasant. Possibly. More likely, however, is that 'nitty-gritty' is simply a rhyming duplication like teeny-weeny or rumpy-pumpy.

KICK THE BUCKET (UK)
Die

Whatever the vicissitudes and drudgeries of the daily grind, they are preferable to the thing that ends them all. Or, as the novelist Henry James was reputed to have remarked on his deathbed, 'So it has come at last, the distinguished thing'. Although there are plenty of slang expressions and idioms to describe death by judicial execution, there are few when it comes to natural death. Jonathon Green, the lexicographer of slang, notes that it may simply be too serious a subject. One term that is not serious, however, is 'kick the bucket'.

This faintly disrespectful metaphor has existed in English for well over two centuries, although there is no general agreement on its source. A derivation which is almost certainly false visualises an individual, whether a suicide or a condemned man, standing on a bucket with a noose around his neck. When the bucket is kicked away, he dies. This seems implausible, if only because a bucket is unlikely to have been standard equipment in such a situation, certainly not frequently enough to produce the saying. A slightly more convincing explanation refers to the bucket of holy water placed by the feet of a dying person, in old Roman Catholic practice. An alternative definition of bucket as a 'beam' or 'yoke' from which things are hung gives the probable answer. This is an old sense of the word, one used by Shakespeare when he has Falstaff in *Henry IV* refer to a worker operating a counterweight on a 'brewer's bucket' (i.e. beam) as part of the brewing process. In a different context, when an animal was slaughtered it would be hung by its heels. In its death throes it might kick against the beam or 'bucket' from which it was suspended. Hence the expression..?

'Kick the bucket' is sometimes described as a euphemism but, if anything, it is an anti-euphemism since its flippancy suggests the user doesn't care much about the person whose death is in question unless, of course, it is said as a robust way of referring to one's own. Although seeming a quintessential English idiom, 'kick the bucket' has been found in the United States at least since the later part of the 19th century and recently gave rise to the unlovely phrase 'bucket list', a wish-list of things to do before death.

TIME, DATES AND NUMBERS

There are few more telling reminders of the unremitting nature of everyday life, of the daily grind, than the relatively new expression 'twenty-four-seven' (or, more usually, '24/7'), signifying 'all the time, day and night'. This very familiar phrase probably emerged from US prison slang in the 1980s. A variant is 24/24, and a longer but rarely seen version is 24-7-365. The formula saves time as well as space. How else could you express the concept of some activity, facility or amenity which is accessible by day and night, uninterruptedly, from New Year's Day until New Year's Eve, without resorting to a long-winded paraphrase like the one in this sentence? 'Round the clock' is the equivalent but belongs the old world of clock faces, hands and even Roman numerals.

The creeping digital intrusion on British English is not much noticed. It gained a bigger foothold with the 9/11 attacks on New York and the Pentagon. Would the abbreviation of that notorious date have caught on as a piece of global shorthand if the Americans used the British system of dating, putting the day before the month (11/9) rather than the other way about? Perhaps not, since the US formula trips more neatly off the tongue. In the United States, the 9/11 formula was made even more memorable by its use as the national emergency telephone number (the equivalent of the UK 999). The London bombings of July 2005 produced the imitative shorthand form of 7/7. The use of numbers in preference to words is also seen in the newish cliché 'from day one' instead of 'from the beginning' or some similar way off expressing the idea. The punchier, more eye-catching language of advertising may also demand figures as well as words, as with the creation of the 7-Eleven franchise immediately after the Second World War (or World War Two, or WW2) or other retail slogans like '8 till late'.

Chapter 7

BIRDS, BEASTS AND BUGS

It's unsurprising that so many idioms concern animals: after all, the animal kingdom has long been a favourite metaphorical domain for commenting on the human world, or more particularly for lampooning human foibles. At the root of this phenomenon is a perceived kinship with other species, an aspect of the pathetic fallacy that manifests itself most obviously in our constant tendency to anthropomorphise their behaviour.

Aesop starts the ball rolling in the 6th century BC, with fables drawing morals for human interaction from encounters between animals. By the 1st century AD the observational approach of Pliny the Elder in his *Natural History* represents the beginnings of zoology, though his comments are still replete with anthropomorphic assumptions: *'Owing to their modesty, elephants never mate except in secret... Adultery is unknown among them'* (Book 8.5.13). In their turn, the authors of medieval bestiaries elicit from beasts' habits all kinds of lessons regarding the ways of God, the Devil and Man. Most famously, the 'Pelican in Its Piety' (which according to a fable, originally from India, killed its young in a fit of anger and then remorsefully brought them back to life with drops of blood produced by pecking open its own breast) symbolised the Passion of Christ.

In the idiomatic realm, to take the case of 'pigs might fly', it's fascinating to see the range of fauna that other languages use to express the same idea – French: *Quand les poules auront des dents* ('When hens have teeth'); Italian: *Quando volerano gli asini*

('When donkeys fly'); Spanish: *Cuando las ranas críen pelo* ('When frogs grow hair'); Finnish: *Kun lehmät lentävät* ('When cows fly'); Portuguese: *Quando a vaca tussa* ('When a cow coughs'); and Turkish: *Balık agaca çikinca* ('When fish climb trees').

A happy hunting ground, then, for the idiom collector...

HAVE THE COCKROACH (French)
Avoir le cafard - **to be down in the dumps/in a black mood**

There's an undisputed literary background to this idiom – most commentators cite Charles Baudelaire's sonnet 'Destruction', from the collection *Les Fleurs du Mal* of 1857. But we must straight away add the caveat that Baudelaire was not referring to cockroaches in his famous work. The lines in question run:

Et, sous de spécieux prétextes de cafard,
Accoutume ma lèvre à des philtres infâmes.

which have been translated as:

And, with pretexts specious and hypocritical,
Accustoms my lips to infamous philtres.

Un cafard (from the Arabic *kafr*, 'unbeliever') originally meant a religious hypocrite, whose faith was a mere sham. In the same way that *Les Fleurs du Mal* popularised the English 'spleen' in France as a synonym for melancholy, Baudelaire's usage of this word was the first occasion on which it was associated with black despair. But *cafard* is also an alternative word for cockroach (the more common being *blatte*, from the order Blattidae) – the connection is that, like hypocrites, cockroaches shun the light, going about their nefarious business in dark corners.

It is this graphic entomological link that has lodged in the popular imagination; other explanations of the phrase bypass Baudelaire entirely, relating the ennui and suicidal gloom that famously affected French Foreign Legionnaires to the cockroaches which infested the remote tropical and subtropical outposts where they served. The idiom must also have called to mind the earlier *avoir le bourdon* ('to have the bumblebee'), another way of saying that you're down in the mouth. Both, incidentally, are now outdated.

Two interesting parallels: German has a similarly outmoded phrase: *Grillen fangen* (literally 'to catch crickets'), meaning to entertain dark thoughts, while Samuel Johnson and Winston Churchill both referred to their own bouts of depression as 'the black dog'.

BLUE DOG (US)

A Democrat politician in the United States who is on the conservative rather than the liberal wing of his party, particularly on fiscal matters

There are several strands to the phrase 'blue dog Democrat'. One goes back to the late 19th century and a newspaper boast from a Democrat that victory in a forthcoming election was so certain that 'we could nominate yellow dogs this Spring and elect every one upon the ticket by a big majority'. Henceforth, the vaguely disparaging term 'yellow dog' described a stalwart, loyal member of the Democratic party. Jump forward a century to the 1990s after the same party had lost control of Congress during Bill Clinton's first presidency, to a moment when a group of centrist Democrats was meeting in the offices of two Louisiana representatives. On their walls hung paintings by a faux-naif Cajun artist depicting a (literally) blue dog – a chihuahua, as it happens. The unofficial grouping may have been inspired by these paintings, as well as by the belief that conservative Democrats were being choked off by a liberal leadership and so turning blue. The Blue Dogs' own website refers to a similar sense of exclusion to explain their blue-dog mascot: 'when dogs are not let into the house, they stay outside in the cold and turn blue.' Blue is also the colour associated with the Democrats, as red is with the Republicans, a reversal of the standard European linkage of blue with right-leaning political parties and red with left-leaning ones.

'Blue dogs' is recognisable shorthand in the US print and digital media to characterise those politicians who adhere to traditional middle-American values but who describe themselves as 'not supporting' gun control, abortion or gay marriage rather than being clamorously against those hot-button causes, as traditional right-wingers would be. It's an interesting example of how rapidly an idiomatic phrase can catch on if it answers a purpose or two. 'Blue dogs' carries a note of contempt and rejection (by a liberal Washington establishment at the top of the Democratic party) as well as the capacity for snarling aggression. The increasingly polarised nature of recent US politics suggests the importance of these tinted canines will grow.

'TROY'/SOW (Italian)

Troia – **prostitute/whore/slut/slag**

A curious case of conflicting, yet ultimately converging, etymologies. In Italian, Troia as a proper noun (capitalised) denotes the historic city in Anatolia whose siege and destruction by the Greeks is recounted in epic poems such as Homer's *Iliad* and Virgil's *Aeneid*. As a general noun (uncapitalised), it means 'sow' (in some regions of Italy, at least) and is, by extension, a deeply insulting term for a woman of ill repute. What link could there possibly be?

Let's take the most direct approach first. This posits no connection with pigs, but instead goes straight to the heart of the ancient myth. The spark that ignited the Trojan War was the seduction of the beautiful Helen, wife of King Menelaus of Sparta, by the Trojan prince Paris. As Christopher Marlowe famously expressed it in *Doctor Faustus* (1604): 'Was this the face that launched a thousand ships/And burnt the topless towers of Ilium?'. The ancient sources are ambiguous about whether Helen was complicit in her abduction. But the clear implication in the modern Italian slang word (if we are to believe this etymology) is that she was: Helen (who by a process of metonymy becomes 'Troy') is thereby condemned as the archetypal 'whore' for deserting her husband and taking up with another man.

Now for the more scenic route. At lavish banquets in Imperial Rome, a dish of whole spit-roasted pig stuffed with successively smaller animals was known as *porcus troianus* ('Trojan pig'), a whimsical allusion to the Trojan horse. By analogy, it may be that *troia* came to mean 'sow' from the fact that the female pig is usually a substantial beast whose bulk makes it appear stuffed even when it's still alive. Common parlance then took up the word for a female animal as a disparaging term for a woman, just as English has done with 'bitch' or 'cow'.

Whatever the true origin of the term, its offensiveness can be ratcheted up a notch, as so often in Italian, by prefacing it with the noun *porca* (as in, say, *Porca miseria!*). This yields the curious phrase *Porca troia* (literally 'sow sow'), which is about as grossly insulting as it gets. Ditto *Porca puttana* (the more common term for whore), though this, depending on context, may be more of a strong interjection than a personal insult, equivalent to 'oh fucking hell!'.

Wisely, Wolfgang Petersen's 2004 film *Troy*, starring Brad Pitt and Orlando Bloom, retained its English title on release in Italy.

JUMP THE SHARK (US)

To perform an action which is so out of place or preposterous that it undermines the credibility of everything which follows it

This bizarre expression dates from a particular episode of the 1970s TV series *Happy Days* in which a character known as The Fonz (played by Henry Winkler) accepted a bet to water ski over a marine enclosure containing a shark. He won the bet but the episode was widely derided as the moment at which the highly successful show began to run out of ideas, with writers and producers scrabbling for ever more extreme ways of holding onto their audience. It was hardly the end for *Happy Days,* which ran for several more years. Nevertheless, the phrase was gleefully adopted not just to poke fun at television shows past their prime but to describe a serious misjudgement or tipping point from which there is little chance of making a recovery. 'Jumping the shark', which can be applied retrospectively, may occur in contexts as diverse as US President Jimmy Carter's wearing of a cardigan during a 1977 TV address in which he advised the nation to turn down the thermostats because of a steep hike in oil prices, or to Lady

Gaga's 2011 appearance at an awards ceremony dressed up as her male alter ego.

The concept tends to crop up in media and new technology commentaries since the hip, knowing quality of the phrase confers insider status on the user. An analagous expression is 'lose the plot' while another but rather more far-fetched parallel is 'nuke the fridge'. This comes from an episode early in the film *Indiana Jones and the Kingdom of the Crystal Skull* (2008), in which Harrison Ford's character escapes a nuclear detonation by climbing into a kitchen fridge (conveniently labelled as lead-lined) which is then blown hundreds of feet through the air. What a surprise it is when Indy emerges from the fridge with no sign of injury!

DO SOMEONE A BEAR SERVICE (GERMAN)

Jemandem einen Bärendienst erweisen – **With friends like you, who needs enemies?**

It may be axiomatic that ursids defecate in the woods, but it's far from clear what a 'bear service' might be. The short answer is: a disservice, albeit unintentional. In German, it denotes a state of affairs where the recipient of a 'favour' is left wishing heartily that the doer of the deed really hadn't bothered.

The idiom has a readily traceable literary source. In a fable by the 17th-century French writer Jean de la Fontaine entitled *L'ours et l'amateur des jardins*, a bear and a gardener decide that they are tired of leading solitary lives and agree to team up. For a while, this symbiotic relationship goes swimmingly, with the bear exercising his special skill of catching game in the woods, while the man tends his vegetable plot. Until the bear notices one day that a fly has landed on his friend's face as he is taking a nap and is in danger of disturbing him:

And so one day when one of those
Annoying parasites lit smack upon the nose
Of the old man as he was taking his siesta –
It was the stinging kind, a most egregious pest, a
Vicious thing – the bear got mad. "I'll fix it good!"
The stout flycatcher said. "And this is how I'll do it!"
With that, he grabbed a boulder with his forepaws, stood
On his hind legs and, using all his strength, he threw it,
Straight downward, managing in the event to smush
The fly and, with good aim and rotten logic, crush
His poor friend's skull and lay him out in rigor mortis.

Doh! This particular beast clearly wasn't smarter than the average bear. The moral that La Fontaine draws from his tale is: *Rien n'est si dangereux qu'un ignorant ami; Mieux vaudroit un sage ennemi* ('An ignorant friend can often be/More dangerous than one's most determined enemy').

Italian conveys a similar meaning in the phrase *Dai nemici mi guardo io, dagli amici mi guardi Iddio!* ('I can protect myself against my enemies, but may God protect me against my friends!').

PIG IN A POKE (UK)

An item bought without being looked at; a commitment made without examination

The pig in the poke is closely related to the cat in the bag (indeed, the German equivalent is 'to buy the cat in the bag': *die Katze im Sack kaufen*). 'Poke' once meant bag or sack, and is still US slang for wallet. It's also a familiar term in Scotland, especially for the paper bag chips are served in: Iain Banks uses it in this sense in his 1992 novel *The Crow*

Road, for example. There was an old market trick of selling a cat in a sack instead of the suckling pig which it should contain. That the trick has a long history is shown by a medieval proverb which translates as 'When someone gives you a pig, then open the pouch'. In contemporary use, buying or accepting a pig in a poke doesn't necessarily entail a swindle. It is more of a warning to the buyer to check the goods beforehand, like the Latin warning *caveat emptor.* If the buyers didn't bother to check but waited until getting home before opening the 'poke', then they might find themselves the protagonists of another idiomatic expression: those who 'let the cat out of the bag'. Presumably the animal was already slaughtered since the presence of a live cat in the bag would be evident to any purchaser after a few moments. It has sometimes been suggested that letting the cat out of the bag refers to the old naval practice of flogging with the cat-o'-nine tails, which would be produced out of the canvas bag in which it was stored before the ritual administration of the brutal punishment. But this half-plausible explanation does not really fit the meaning of the phrase, which is to give away something secret.

The expression 'to buy a pup' might appear to be connected to pigs and cats in pokes and bags, since it means that the buyer has been short-changed or swindled. Certainly, it's easy to imagine a less squeamish era in which puppies in sacks might be passed off as more valuable animals. But the 'sell/buy a pup' expression is not recorded until the start of the 20th century, far too late for it to have any medieval source. The allusion is either to the fact that the pup has be trained, so that most of the effort and expense fall on the purchaser, or that its value is prospective rather than actual.

BREAK A BUTTERFLY ON A WHEEL (UK)
Put great effort into accomplishing something insignificant

Breaking a butterfly on a wheel sounds comparatively innocent, perhaps reflecting the moment when a Red Admiral or a Cabbage White is inadvertently crushed under the tyre of some vehicle. But its origins are rather darker. The creator of the phrase was the 18th-century satirical poet Alexander Pope, who imagines one of his friends asking why he goes to such trouble to attack trivial figures, surely the equivalent of breaking a butterfly on a wheel. The 'butterfly' allusion is to one of Pope's particular targets, a bisexual royal courtier while the 'wheel' refers to an instrument of execution in Europe and elsewhere. It was one of the most brutal forms of punitive capital punishment ever devised. When he was to be broken in such a fashion, the condemned individual was pinned to a wagon wheel to have his limbs shattered with a hammer or cudgel before being left to die at his own pace. It is this macabre contrast, between the fragility of the butterfly and a remorseless method of public execution, which Pope is deploying in his metaphor.

Curiously, the French expression *roué*, quite widely used in English and meaning a 'dissolute person' or 'rake', also harks back to being broken on a wheel (one of the senses of the verb *rouer*). The term was used by a French nobleman about his debauched companions, as if they were deserving of a worse punishment than that given to ordinary lower-class criminals who would merely be hanged. Applications of *roué* now tend to be milder, indeed almost affectionate, and are often preceded by 'old'. In the same way, the gruesome associations of breaking a butterfly on a wheel, which would have been familiar to Alexander Pope and his contemporaries, are unknown or forgotten.

HAVE A SPIDER ON THE CEILING (French)

Avoir une araignée au plafond – **to have a screw loose**

Colloquialisms abound in many languages to describe people who aren't dangerously deranged, but instead are touched, eccentric, flaky. Animal metaphors are common in this department: we need only think of the English terms 'to have bats in the belfry,' or 'to have a bee in your bonnet'. German, similarly, speaks of a person 'having a bird' (*einen Vogel haben*). The force of all of these is clear, evoking the erratic, unpredictable movements of mammals, insects or birds trapped in a confined space.

But the most intriguing beasts on the brain are spiders. Confined spaces are where they naturally hang out, and their actions are anything but erratic. They spend their time methodically spinning intricate, symmetrical, beautiful webs; in the late 1940s, scientists discovered that the only way to put these master weavers off their stroke was to dose them with stimulants like mescaline or LSD – or indeed caffeine, which resulted in the most chaotic webs of all. French isn't the only language to associate spiders with benign madness: German uses the verb *spinnen* to describe crazy behaviour (ultimately deriving from the word for a spider, *eine Spinne*), and calls an oddball or crank a *Spinner*.

What's being appositely symbolised here is the obsessive and repetitive nature of the eccentric's thought patterns. The grey-bearded loon who holds you with his glittering eye generally has an *idée fixe*, an abiding obsession that fills his every waking moment – be it abduction by aliens, persecution by the local council, or a conviction that the 1969 Moon landing was faked. The round-and-round-and-roundness of such manias – even more apparent if we call to mind the extended meaning of 'to spin', as in 'spinning yarn' or 'spinning wheel' – is also captured by a more recent French idiom expressing the same idea: *avoir un petit vélo dans la tête* – 'to have a little bicycle in the head'.

NOT ENOUGH ROOM TO SWING A CAT IN
(UK)

Cramped

That brutal flogging implement which was once used in the British navy, the cat-o'-nine tails, is responsible for two false etymologies. One is letting the cat out of the bag (see **Pig in a poke**), while the other is the familiar characterisation of some indoor space as being too small 'to swing a cat in'. According to this interpretation, the man with the flogger/cat-o'-nine tails needs a bit of elbow room to wield it effectively. As often, a bit of historical dating does for the most straightforward explanation. The earliest recorded appearance of 'not space enough to swing a cat in', which is glossed as 'a vulgar saying' (i.e. one used by ordinary people), occurs in 1665 and that is long before the appearance of the dreaded cat-o'-nine tails. It is quite likely that the phrase refers to the actual swinging of an actual cat, recalling the days when mistreatment of animals was more routine and accepted than it is now. Shakespeare must have been familiar with swinging the cat since in *Much Ado about Nothing*, he has Benedick deny that he will ever fall in love with the words: 'If I do, hang me in a bottle like a cat, and shoot at me.' The allusion is to archers aiming at cats stuffed into bags or canteen-like bottles made of leather which were then dangled from branches for target practice. An alternative possibility is that, since 'cat' was a slang word for a rogue among many other things, the reference might be to a felon swinging or hanging from the gallows. The sensible money, though, would be on the feline.

NO TRIPE FOR CATS! (ITALIAN)

Non c'è trippa per gatti – **No chance!/Not a snowball's chance in Hell!**

Lounging all over the ancient sites of Rome are hordes of feral cats of every size and hue. The Largo di Torre Argentina, scene of Julius Caesar's assassination, teems with them (there's a cat sanctuary on the square), while in the Colosseum, where Barbary lions from Numidia and Mauretania once mauled prisoners of war and Christians (in a bloodthirsty entertainment called 'exposure to the beasts'), mogs now prowl, stalking your packed lunch. Such a familiar sight are they that tourists can even buy a calendar of the 'Gatti di Roma', showing, say, a tiny tabby perched gracefully on the big toe of a massive stone foot, the remains of a gargantuan piece of statuary from the Baths of Caracalla.

Nowadays, well-meaning ladies of a certain age cater to the felines' food needs, but up to a century or so ago they were on the city's payroll. The municipality used to regularly dole out offal to the strays, which were seen as providing a useful service by keeping down vermin. Until, that is, one Ernesto Nathan became mayor in 1907. Reviewing the city's budget, he was amazed to find the offal and its cost itemised there and, scrawling the immortal phrase in the ledger, immediately cut off the supply. Nathan's injunction soon got taken up as a rejoinder to anyone whose hopes or expectations you meant to dash.

Robert Frost famously defined poetry as 'what gets lost in translation'. It applies equally to idioms. At the Champions League football final in Athens in May 2007, a group of AC

Milan fans, wishing to taunt their rivals from Liverpool, unfurled a banner with this strange device: 'No Tripe for Cats!' Wonder how many of the assembled Scousers got the message?

LAME DUCK (UK)

A bankrupt individual/person lacking power to act

The world of high finance provides some vivid expressions with animal connections such as 'dead cat bounce' (a small but illusory rise in share prices after a large fall, and sometimes called a 'sucker's rally' in the United States) or the 'bull' and 'bear' terms characterising different types of speculator and markets. A bull market – as symbolised by the statue of the imposing animal which is to be seen near Wall Street – is buoyed up by rising prices and presumably draws on the potent, aggressive image of the animal. A bear market, by contrast, is one in which stocks are sinking, and may derive from fur traders who sold their supplies in the expectation that prices would drop.

These financial creatures were alluded to in a letter from the 18th-century writer and dilettante Horace Walpole, who asked his correspondent: 'Do you know what a Bull, and a Bear, and a Lame Duck are?' This is the earliest known mention (1761) of a 'lame duck', and later references also connect the limping bird to the stock exchange ('Change-Alley bankrupts waddle out lame ducks!'). Even without the implied comparison to the thunderous motion of the bull or the stamp of the bear, there is something comic about the duck's movement on dry land, and no doubt this is behind the reference, together with the vulnerability implied by lameness. The term was much used in Britain in the 1970s to signal the government's reluctance to give state subsidies to 'lame duck' industries such as car- and shipbuilders, which were seen as inefficient or outmoded in the way they operated. When applied to an individual, 'lame duck' indicates ineffectiveness, usually of a person in a position of would-be authority. In the United States, the expression has a political application to describe an office holder whose power is reduced because he or she is about to step down. The most obvious example is the period of roughly 10 weeks which falls between the early November elections for US President and, if the incumbent is defeated or has already served two terms of office, the inauguration of his successor in the following year on 20th January.

COMBING THE GIRAFFE (French)
Peigner la girafe – **to waste time on a pointless task**

The first giraffe to set foot on French soil was a female by the name of Zarafa, which was sent in 1826 as a gift to King Charles X (r.1824–30) by the Pasha of Egypt, Muhammad Ali (who also gave giraffes to George IV and the Holy Roman Emperor Francis II in the same year). After overwintering in Marseilles, in the late spring of the following year the animal was led on foot to Paris on an 800-kilometre journey lasting 41 days, and caused a sensation at every town she passed through. Zarafa arrived in the French capital on 30 June 1827, was presented to the king and installed in a special enclosure in the Jardin des Plantes. She survived for another 18 years, outliving both the king (who was deposed in 1830 and died six years later) and the naturalist Étienne Geoffroy Saint-Hilaire, who was responsible for Zarafa's welfare during her trek to Paris.

Accompanying Saint-Hilaire and the giraffe was a team of four keepers, one of whom was tasked solely with grooming her coat with a curry comb. One school of thought traces the origin of the expression directly to this humble, unnamed giraffe-hand. The popularity of Zarafa – 100,000 people, or one-eighth of population of Paris at the time, came to see her – makes it entirely plausible that all the minutiae of her care should have become the subject of comment, including this long, tedious, but ultimately quite cushy job of work. So, with nuances of both 'nice work if you can get it' and 'painting the Forth Bridge', *peigner la girafe* may have entered the French language there and then as the epitome of a pointless occupation.

But there's another meaning to the phrase that may make all this historical speculation a pointless task in itself. It's a euphemism for masturbation; it doesn't take a Sigmund Freud to spot the superficial similarity between the extraordinarily long neck of *Giraffa camelopardalis* and the erect male member. The connection between this activity and uselessness is that a person who indulges in it to excess may be deemed to be frittering away time better spent on gainful tasks; proponents of this explanation cite the abusive term *peigne-zizi* (literally 'prick-comber', meaning a 'fuckwit' or 'useless tosser') as a clear analogy.

This second interpretation gained ground after some commentators confidently declared there to be no known occurrences of the phrase (in either sense) before 1945. But in 1990, Claude Duneton (in his work on idioms, *La Puce à l'oreille*) scotched the masturbation theory by unearthing a reference to the idiom as a term for 'doing nothing' in the 1898 edition of the *Nouveau Larousse Illustré* dictionary.

Serenely oblivious to all this controversy and vulgarity, Zarafa, who was stuffed in 1845, now graces the first-floor landing of the Museum of Natural History in the western port of La Rochelle.

SCREW THE POOCH (US)

To waste time/make a serious mistake

'Screw the pooch' is slang usage verging on what dictionaries call 'vulgar'. It is a euphemism, though not much of one, for 'fuck the dog' or, in more polite society, 'fornicate the poodle', both of which make their appearance in the United States soon after the start of the 20th century. Although the original meaning of these expressions was to loaf about, to do nothing of productive use, the variant form 'screw the pooch' was popularised by Tom Wolfe in his book *The Right Stuff* (1979) about test pilots and the postwar programme which led to the first space flights. By this stage the expression had mutated and turned into something much more serious than mere idling. Now it describes a grave error, even a catastrophic one. Wolfe describes a test pilot as 'screwing the pooch' and goes on to explain: 'In flight tests, if you did something that stupid, if you destroyed a major prototype, through some lame-brain mistake such as hitting the wrong button – you were through!' 'Screwing the pooch' should not be confused with 'shooting the puppy', an item of macho business-speak which means to do something that is both ruthless and necessary.

YOU CAN'T PLUCK FEATHERS FROM A BALD FROG (DUTCH)

Van een kale kicker kan je geen veren plukken – **a pointless exercise/trying to get blood from a stone**

A straightforward enough idiom, but with some interesting multilingual tangents to go off on. A more impossible and pointless task is scarcely imaginable: trying to find feathers to pluck on the smooth and slippery skin of a frog. Much the same idea is conveyed by the Spanish idiom *Cuando las ranas crien pelo* ('When frogs grow hair'), which has the sense of 'when hell freezes over' or 'never in a month of Sundays'.

German has a slightly different slant on this particular idiomatic use of frogs. *Jemandem zeigen, wo der Frosch die Locken hat* – 'to show someone where the frog has curls [of hair]' – is a phrase meaning 'to show someone what's what/ how to do it.' The suggestion is that, as an expert, you'll even have the knack of teaching people seemingly impossible tricks.

A synonymous phrase with the one above is *Jemandem zeigen, wo der Hammer hängt* ('to show someone where the hammer's hanging'), the reference here obviously being to competent workmanship and tools. This one's of interest because of its proximity to the current bloke-ish American man-to-man greeting 'How's your hammer hanging?' (often abbreviated to 'How's it hanging?'). All it means is 'How are you?' but obviously alludes to genitalia. Is it too far-fetched to imagine that the original idiom was imported to the United States by German immigrants, where in time it metamorphosed from an innocent phrase concerning know-how and skill into a jocular enquiry about sexual prowess?

ALL HAT AND NO CATTLE (US)
Describing someone who presents himself as important, rich etc., but whose claims are doubtful or without substance

This US expression is constructed along the familiar 'All ... and no ...' formula in which the second part undercuts the first, always to the detriment of whatever is being described ('All talk and no action', 'All sizzle and no steak', 'All bark and no bite', 'All fur coat and no knickers'). The wide-open ranges of the American West are the obvious source for the hat and the herd, with the swagger of the Stetson set against the fact that its wearer doesn't possess the cattle that ought to go with it. The expression seems to be of fairly recent origin. A *New York Times* article of 1984 puts the phrase in inverted commas, a sign that it was not really in mainstream use at the time, while more recent references appear without marks or as a compound adjective; 'all-hat-no-cattle'. In 1999, Randy Newman issued a song in a faux country-and-western style entitled 'Big Hat, No Cattle'.

Despite some overlap of meaning, there is no connection to the older and slightly baffling British expression 'All mouth and trousers', which hails from the north of England and which is a put-down of male boastfulness. This more usually appears now in the negative version of 'All mouth and no trousers', a distortion which probably comes from the 'all... and no...' formula as well as the humiliation of being caught without trousers on. Anyone wanting to avoid mouths and trousers altogether could once have turned to the Victorian equivalent of 'gas and gaiters'.

THAT DOESN'T FIT ON ANY COW HIDE
(GERMAN)

That's beyond the pale/that beggars belief

Before paper became cheaply available in Europe (from the 12th century onwards, spreading from Byzantium), parchment was the writing material of choice for early medieval scribes. The word comes from the Greek *pergamene*, meaning 'of Pergamon', the ancient city in Asia Minor whose ruler

Eumenes II (r. 197–159 BC) is credited with expanding the Great Library. Eumenes is also reputed to have developed parchment manufacture on an industrial scale to get around an embargo on the export of papyrus-based paper imposed by Ptolemy VI of Egypt, who feared the growth of a rival seat of learning to the Royal Library of Alexandria. The finest form of parchment was vellum, made from the skins of young animals such as calves, kids or lambs.

There was a widespread belief in medieval Christianity that the Devil kept a tally of a person's transgressions during their life on a piece of parchment. This he would unroll before miserable sinners while leading them down to Hell. Some surviving wall paintings in Germany and elsewhere attest to this legend; the 10th-century Church of St George in Oberzell on the island of Reichenau on Lake Constance, for instance, has a fresco showing four demons stretching out a parchment, while another registers the idle chit-chat of two women (pictured in the background) on the roll call of dishonour. The didactic message couldn't be more obvious: don't gossip in church. Anyone whose sins wouldn't even fit on the hide of a fully-grown cow, however large, was clearly destined for damnation.

ALBATROSS AROUND ONE'S NECK (UK)
A burden/handicap

The expression 'having/wearing an albatross about one's neck' is quite often found, reduced to a simple reference to the bird. ('But that's fine, I don't see it as an albatross'). That a large seabird from the southern hemisphere became synonymous with a personal burden is the responsibility of the poet Samuel Taylor Coleridge. In *The Rime of the Ancient Mariner* (1798), the old seaman of the title tells how his shipmates turned on him after he shot an albatross with a crossbow. The ship is becalmed and the superstitious sailors blame the mariner:

> *Ah! well a-day! what evil looks*
> *Had I from old and young!*
> *Instead of the cross, the Albatross*
> *About my neck was hung.*

The albatross eventually falls from the mariner's neck, but he remains haunted by the story as well as obsessed by the need to tell others of his experience. It is an odd story, and almost as odd is that apart from a single reference in Mary Shelley's novel *Frankenstein* (1818) – and Mary and Percy Shelley were friends of Coleridge – more than 150 years were to pass before the albatross-round-the-neck became established in the language as a metaphor. Yet now British and American newspaper sites will throw up dozens of examples, even in truncated form like 'albatross contracts' or with variants such as 'getting at least one albatross off their backs'. One reason for its resonance may be that the word carries an echo of 'cross', also denoting a burden. In general use, the albatross metaphor has largely flown away from its guilty connotations to become the simple equivalent of an awkward and perhaps inescapable problem. In the same way, the comparable metaphor of a millstone round the neck has become synonymous with a weight one must carry rather than the more threatening sense conveyed by its biblical context, when Christ warned that 'whoso shall offend one of these little ones which believe in me, it were better for him that a millstone were hanged about his neck, and that he were drowned in the depth of the sea' (Matthew 19:6).

LIKE BURIDAN'S ASS (FRENCH)

Comme l'âne de Buridan – **to be in a quandary**

Even if we're not able to give a succinct definition of them, many of us have heard of Schrödinger's cat or Occam's razor. Less familiar to us is Buridan's ass.

Jean Buridan (c.1300–c.1358) was a French philosopher and scientist who developed a theory of impetus that anticipated the concept of inertia in modern physics. Yet it's another form of inertia that is the subject of the most famous idea associated with him: the ass (or donkey). You'd search in vain for it in his writings, though; it was invented by those who aimed to ridicule his concept of moral determinism. In discussing this matter, Buridan worked from the premise that there is no distinction between faculties of the soul such as the will and intellect. Faced with a situation where the will presents two alternative courses of action as equally desirable, Buridan's position should logically mean that there can be no choice. The philosopher's way out of this paradox was to claim that the will could postpone its decision so as to fully assess the possible outcomes of the choice. His conclusion was that a human faced with two must inevitably choose the greater good.

This is just as unconvincing as Dr. Pangloss's naïve optimism ('everything is for the best in the best of all possible worlds') in Voltaire's *Candide*. Buridan's opponents introduced the satirical image of the ass to point this out – positioned midway between a pail of water and a bale of hay, it can never come to a rational decision to choose one over the other, and ends up starving to death.

Latterly, divested of all the quibbling distinctions of medieval scholasticism, Buridan's ass became a powerful image of fatal indecision. A US satirical cartoon from the turn of the 20th century showed Congress as Buridan's ass, havering endlessly between a route through Nicaragua or Panama for the proposed canal linking the Atlantic and the Pacific.

Quakers also took the donkey/bales of hay image and, sidestepping the niceties of moral philosophy and the question of the existence of free will, used it to make a telling social point about enlightened altruism. Under the heading *'The Two Mules: Co-operation is Better than Conflict'*, a famous poster produced by the Society of Friends showed the beasts, which are joined by a too-short length of rope, fruitlessly pulling in opposite directions to get at piles of hay beyond their reach. Only when they pool their resources and walk together to share each bale in turn is their predicament resolved.

AT ONE FELL SWOOP (UK)
With great suddenness

Metaphors and idioms have a life of their own, subject to mutations that were never thought of by their originators (in those cases where an originator can be pinned down). Like the coins or notes of a currency, they get rubbed or creased with age so that verbal details become obscured, especially when the idiom gets written down. For example, the phrase 'damp squib', to describe some event which doesn't go off with the expected bang, is frequently rendered as 'damp squid', presumably through some association between wetness and undersea creatures, and because more people can visualise a squid than they can a squib (a 16th-century term for a firework). To the 'manner born' is often written as to the 'manor born', while 'praying mantis' may come out as 'preying mantis'. These changes make a kind of sense: a person behaving as 'to the manner born' probably carries the air of entitlement that comes with being born in a manor; and the mantis, described as 'praying' because it carries its forelegs in an attitude of prayer, is also highly predatory. In similar style, 'fell swoop' may emerge as 'fowl swoop', 'foul swoop', and other variations. But the 'correct' version is the first.

Shakespeare has the earliest recorded use in *Macbeth*, when Macduff hears that his entire family has been slaughtered by Macbeth's men in an act of murderous spite:

> *All my pretty ones?*
> *Did you say all? O hell-kite! All?*
> *What, all my pretty chickens and their dam*
> *At one fell swoop?*

Macbeth is the hell-kite. The kite, a bird of prey regarded in Shakespeare's day as little better than a carrion bird but one which is now being carefully reintroduced into the United Kingdom, swoops down on its prey with a distinctive but deadly sideways motion. The 'fell' in 'fell swoop' has nothing to do with the way it drops from the sky but draws on an almost forgotten sense of 'fell', meaning 'cruel'. Shakespeare again uses it like this when he has Hamlet refer to 'this fell sergeant death' moments before he dies. Going back to the 'incorrect' versions of the metaphor, 'at one fowl swoop' and 'at one foul swoop', one could argue that while the 'fowl' version might suggest a chicken plunging out of the skies, the 'foul' one catches something of the original ruthlessness of the expression. Even when mangled, metaphors can still do their job.

LET'S RETURN TO OUR SHEEP (FRENCH)

Revenons à nos moutons – **to get back to the matter in hand/
As I was saying...**

This phrase comes from a play entitled *La Farce de Maistre
Pierre Pathelin*, by an unknown author, which was highly
popular in 15th-century France. François Rabelais is thought
to have drawn on this comedy when writing his ribald works
in the following century.

The farce concerns a court case brought by a clothier called
Guillaume Joceaulme against his shepherd, Thibault l'Aignelet,
whom he accuses of rustling sheep. When the case comes to
trial, Joceaulme immediately recognises the defence counsel, a
local lawyer (Master Pathelin of the title), as someone who
swindled him out of six yards of fine cloth just a few days earlier.
Joceaulme is distracted from his original complaint and keeps
harping on about Pathelin's crime; the judge constantly tries
to bring him back to the matter under consideration with the
words *revenons à nos moutons*. The plaintiff is further frustrated
by l'Aignelet's refusal to say anything but 'Baaa!' in response to
questioning, as instructed by his attorney.

The pleasing rhyme of the phrase saw it become established
as a general way of exhorting someone (or oneself) to get back
to the matter in hand. It was also adopted by English, either
verbatim or as the facetious translation: 'Let's return to our
muttons.'

DOGSBODY (UK)

Someone working at a menial level; a drudge

Beginning as a piece of 19th-century naval slang to describe
pease pudding (peas boiled in a cloth with the addition of sea
biscuit), the term 'dog's-body' was transferred to those who

ate it and came to signify a midshipman, the most junior officer. The original 'dog' metaphor may come from the shape of the pudding as well as the sometimes negative associations of the animal: a dogsbody will probably be leading a dog's life with a dog's chance of getting on. The dogsbody pudding would have been unappetising but there are other and more grotesque navy food terms such as 'boiled baby', describing a kind of suet pudding, or Sweet Fanny Adams (see entry, p.198).

'Dogsbody' joins a list of terms which are used in wry disparagement of the kind of work and worker who is at or near the bottom of the pile. Others include bottle-washer, spear carrier (from the stage actor whose non-speaking job is simply to swell numbers) and jobsworth, used to define the person who enforces rules by prohibiting someone from doing something with the formula 'It's more than my job's worth to let you... '.

THE AMERICAN ELEPHANT

Zoologically, there are just three species of elephant: the Asian, plus two African elephants (the Savanna and the Forest). Idiomatically, we must add to this the American Elephant, first identified in the mid-19th century and still very much alive and well today.

As the United States expanded across the continent to fulfil its 'Manifest Destiny', early pioneers heading west to stake a claim on a farmstead or to try their luck at gold prospecting spoke of 'seeing the elephant' – in other words, having the adventure of a lifetime and experiencing something truly out of the ordinary. The phrase is believed to have come from a story about a farmer taking a wagonload of produce to market in a local town, where he had heard a circus had come to perform. Keen to witness the spectacle, he drove his horse and cart to the circus parade, which was led by an elephant. His horse, however, took fright and bolted, spilling the load of vegetables onto the road and ruining them. The farmer reportedly took the mishap in his stride, announcing: 'I don't give a hang, for I have seen the elephant'.

And so the phrase was used to express a devil-may-care insouciance, a slightly bragging assurance that you'd been round the block a few times, seen some exotic things and knew what was what.

Inevitably, perhaps, it spilled over from this more general usage to signify another kind of adventure into the unknown: the gaining of sexual experience by a young man. By the 1890s, 'seeing the elephant' was a common euphemism for visiting one of the many brothels that abounded throughout the United States, especially in the mining settlements of the Wild West. As so often with idioms, a tributary comes in to join the main river at this point: in 1885, a speculator named James V. Lafferty erected an extraordinary novelty building at the New York beach resort of Coney Island. Standing seven stories high and with 31 rooms, it was in the shape of an enormous Indian elephant with a *howdah* on its back, and was designed as a hotel. As the seaside resort grew increasingly popular and seedy, the 'Elephantine Colossus' gained a reputation as a haunt of prostitutes. So, literal and figurative speech converged where 'seeing the elephant' on Coney Island was concerned. The hotel was destroyed by fire in 1896.

Much more recently, the realm of psychobabble has given us a subspecies of American Elephant known as 'the elephant in the (living) room'. Dating from the mid-1980s, it means a subject that everyone is painfully aware of but is too embarrassed to broach. It has since become a tired journalistic cliché; there's no shortage of comments on the Web wishing that this particular pachyderm would become extinct.

Chapter 8

NATIONAL IDENTITY

It's a pious commonplace to claim that learning languages brings nations closer together, breaks down barriers, makes friends of former foes and so on. This ain't necessarily so. Mark Twain ironically prefaced his 1880 essay 'The Awful German Language' with a quotation from *Proverbs* chapter XXXII, verse VII: 'A little learning makes the whole world kin.' As people master their native language, or reach such an advanced stage in a foreign tongue that they encounter idioms, it soon becomes apparent that there is an abundance of phrases out there tailor-made to offend your neighbour. Perversely, then, some people find that steeping themselves in another language and culture only helps them hone their prejudices to a needle-sharp point. All the better to poke Johnny Foreigner in the eye with.

Here we present some of the more inventive and insulting ways in which nation has spoken unto nation.

SPEAK FRENCH LIKE A SPANISH COW
(FRENCH)

Parler français comme une vache espagnole – **to speak French very badly**

No beating about the bush here. None of the studied cruelty of Parisian shopkeepers who, after letting you stumble through your worst ungrammatical schoolboy French, oleaginously announce: '*Mais Monsieur a une excellente maîtrise du français!*' This tells it like it is: you speak appalling French.

The commonest assumption is that the absurd simile (after all, cows aren't fluent in either French or Spanish, nor – contrary to the claims of certain cheesemakers – do they laugh) is a corruption of 'un(e) Basque espagnol(e)'. 'Basque' comes from the Latin word *vasces* (cognate with 'Gascon'), to describe the ancient inhabitants of far southwestern France and northeastern Spain. The Basque tongue is a language isolate, with no extant relatives on the Indo-European tree. The speakers of this arcane language, especially on the Spanish side of the border, would, then, surely be bound to make a hash of French. The phrase made its first appearance in French dictionaries in the mid-17th century.

The only snag is that this supposed etymology is all pure surmise, with no historical documentation to attest it. A second hypothesis is that the term derives from *baxo* (meaning 'lower'). This makes the slur not one against Basques at all; far from it, in fact. The ethnically and linguistically mixed people of the borderlands were adept at all three languages, whereas the Castilians of the Spanish heartland and others even further south on the Iberian Peninsula could be relied upon to speak bad French.

And yet another school of thought makes the insult one of both race and class, by identifying it as coming from *basse*, an old word for 'servant' (i.e. one of the lower orders). But again, there's scant evidence to support this theory.

This is yet another idiom that has crossed borders. The Dutch say: *Hij kent Frans als een koe Spaans*.

CHINESE WALLS (US)

Imagined barrier existing between different departments of an organisation, intended to avoid conflicts of interest

This is primarily a financial term and describes the policy of non-communication which should exist in certain circumstances between two or more arms of a company to ensure that secret or sensitive information does not leak from one to another. A conflict of interest would arise if inside information about, say, an imminent takeover known to the corporate finance department of a bank were to become available to its investment branch. Similar conflicts could arise if a large legal practice were to represent different parties involved in the same case. Chinese walls are a method of separating the functions of various departments, a virtual barrier to the transmission of information. Although the metaphor is ripe for mockery, so that a particular Chinese wall is said to be full of holes etc., the procedure behind it is supposed to be accountable, even enforceable under the law. Whether it works is another matter. Michael Lewis in *The Big Short*, his book about the 2008 financial crash, quotes a bond trader: 'When I hear "Chinese wall", I think, "You're a fucking liar."'

Contrary to some claims, the term is quite recent. US newspaper references in the 1980s sometimes enclose 'Chinese walls' in quotation marks or preface it with 'so-called' and/or offer an explanation – sure signs that the expression is new. Another misconception is that it derives from the Great Wall of China. A much more likely source is the temporary screens used in the East to demarcate room areas or to provide privacy. The Great Wall was built to keep out hostile tribes and is a physical monument that has endured for millennia. By comparison, Chinese walls or screens are no more than a temporary and figurative means of keeping separate colleagues who work for the same organisation. Nevertheless, the idea of distance and solidity evoked by the image of the Great Wall probably contributes to the popular conception of Chinese walls. There has been some objection in the United States to the phrase because of its ethnic focus. A Californian judge, describing the term as a piece of 'legal flotsam' which should be discarded, pointed out that although the Chinese wall principle is ethically useful it also has negative associations because it signifies a bar to free communication. There are alternatives like 'firewall' or 'ethics wall' but these do not seem to be as popular as the original idiom.

HOLLAND/LEIDEN IS IN TROUBLE! (Dutch)

Dan is Holland/Leiden in last! – **We've got big problems/ we're really up against it!**

The sea is Holland's great friend. The country's enormous prosperity, which peaked in the 17th century, was built on maritime exploration and the founding of a seaborne trading empire. But it's also its worst enemy: almost half of the Netherlands lies below sea level – an area that extends nearly as far as Tilburg in the south and well beyond Zwolle and Groningen, respectively in the centre and north of the country.

The first attested use of the phrase *Dan is Holland in last* is in 1561. The consensus is that this more general form of the idiom (now used ironically) simply refers to the constant threat of inundation. The danger was brought home by the catastrophic North Sea storm surge of January 1953, which overwhelmed sea defences and claimed the lives of 1,835 people, mainly in the southern province of Zeeland.

But what about Leiden? It's plumb in the middle of the danger zone, for sure, but is by no means the most low-lying city in the Netherlands (Amsterdam is six metres below sea level). Here, the reference seems rather to be to an historical event and a threat posed by a human agent. During the 80-year Dutch rebellion against Spanish rule, Leiden was besieged by Spain's Duke of Alba from May to October 1574. Facing imminent capitulation and the starvation of its citizens, the city was saved by the *Stadtholder* and leader of the revolt William the Silent's desperate ploy of destroying the dykes and flooding the province. This allowed a fleet of 200 small ships to sail in and provision the beleaguered city.

The Germans also have a form of the phrase, now rather archaic: *Da ist Holland in Not!* Solicitous concern for their Germanic-speaking cousins to the West, or our old friend *Schadenfreude* rearing its ugly head once more?

MEXICAN STAND-OFF (US)

An unsatisfactory outcome/a deadlock because neither party is willing to back down

In its modern application, the phrase describes a tense confrontation in which each side is equally matched, unable to act but also unable to give way without loss of face. It may be used to characterise a clash between organisations and even countries. The 'Mexican stand-off' is also a cliché in Tarantino-style macho movies, as in a scene when two or more characters simultaneously aim guns at each other's heads. One suggestion for the origin of the phrase dates it as far back as 1845 when the United States and Mexico were engaged in a bitter dispute over the independence of Texas, a dispute which led to the outbreak of war between the two countries in 1846. But the earliest meaning of 'stand-off', emerging at about this period, is a draw or stalemate, while the first dictionary citation of 'Mexican stand-off' is dated towards the end of the 19th century. It seems unlikely that such a long time would have passed between the events which supposedly created the expression and its appearance in print. The most plausible explanation for the phrase is to be found in the easy racial stereotyping it offers. In US slang and informal usage is to be found an almost uniformly derogatory view of Mexico and Mexicans. There are literally dozens of such terms, ranging from a 'Mexican breakfast' (a cigarette and a glass of water) to a 'Mexican jeep' (a donkey). To confirm the disparaging associations of the term, among the now-defunct definitions for 'Mexican stand-off' were a massacre and an execution by firing squad. Because a stand-off is by its nature something unsatisfactory and unresolved, it becomes amplified by the addition of a piece of racial stereotyping.

THE ENGLISH HAVE LANDED (French)

Les Anglais ont débarqué – **to have one's period/ 'time of the month'**

The idiom *les Anglais ont débarqué* is cleverly double-edged (how typical of the French). As a circumlocution, it succeeds on a very basic level in being less offensive than an unadorned statement of fact. But at the same time its clear agenda is to be grossly offensive – certainly to the English, by identifying them with a natural bodily function historically regarded as 'shameful' or 'unclean,' and probably also to women, by belittling their monthly 'curse' with a jocular xenophobic jibe. To coin another phrase, a case of having one's linguistic cake and eating it.

Its origins lie in the Revolutionary and Napoleonic Wars and their aftermath, especially the period (1815–20) following Napoleon's final defeat and the Congress of Vienna, when France found herself occupied by foreign troops. The hated English were easily identified by the bright red coats they wore. One further level of allusion may be that the brutality that the appearance of English soldiers invariably heralded – symbolised in the spilt blood of French soldiers and civilians – was transferred by association to menstrual bleeding. For all its historical resonance, the phrase is still very much alive and well in current French usage, and has even been streamlined to *avoir les Anglais* ('to have the English').

An interesting variation on the theme, which transfers the insult to the Roman Catholic Church and must surely derive from the long tradition of anti-clericalism in France, is *recevoir un courrier de Rome* ('to receive a messenger from Rome'). The clear reference here is to the red of a cardinal's robe.

As a postscript, it's worth pointing out that if we hadn't *débarqué* on 6 June 1944 along with our US and Canadian allies, France would now be *Gau Frankreich*. Bloody French.

PLAY RUSSIAN ROULETTE (US?)
To engage in dangerous, potentially self-destructive behaviour

The literal, non-metaphorical picture of playing Russian roulette is of someone loading a revolver with a single bullet, spinning the chamber and then putting the barrel to his temple and pressing the trigger. On the assumption that the gun has the standard number of chambers, the chances of being shot through the head are one in six. This was the experience described by the writer Graham Greene in his autobiography *A Sort of Life* (1971). Greene claimed that, as a young man in the 1920s, a sense of futility and extreme boredom drove him to risk death in this way after he found a gun belonging to his brother. Survival left him with 'an extraordinary sense of jubilation.' The first citation of Russian roulette in the *Oxford English Dictionary* is dated 1937, when it was used as the title of a short story in the US magazine, *Collier's*. But in the story, by George Surdez, the gun used by the Russian army officers has *five* loaded chambers and only one empty one. If this is the authentic Russian roulette then it is a 'game' in which the odds are so heavily weighted against the holder of the gun that it amounts almost to suicide.

There may, however, be an earlier and undiscovered source since Graham Greene mentions having been given the idea by reading a book – 'I think Ossendowski was the author' – which describes the traditional one-bullet form of Russian roulette, supposedly played among Tsarist Russian officers to stave off boredom. While the roulette part of the phrase is explained by the spinning of the revolver chamber, the Russian associations, whether historically valid or not, depend on the popular image of the nationals of that country as having a penchant for grand but reckless gestures. Whatever the precise source and meaning of the phrase, it is now used almost exclusively in a figurative sense to characterise a perilous situation in which the participants are at risk, not necessarily of losing their lives but of forfeiting something of value through impetuous behaviour.

IT'S ALL SPANISH/BOHEMIAN VILLAGES TO ME (German)

Für mich spanische/böhmische Dörfer sein – **It's all Greek to me/I can't make head nor tail of it**

What could be more unintelligible than a language on which you can gain not the slightest foothold? Citing another language as the epitome of unfathomability appears to be common idiomatic currency, in Europe at least. Most cultures take exotic or difficult tongues with an unfamiliar script as their point of reference. The French, for instance, say *C'est de l'hébreu pour moi* ('That's Hebrew to me' – a direct translation of an Ancient Greek idiom), while Spaniards and Italians light respectively upon Chinese or Aramaic (*Esto me suena a chino/arameo*) and Arabic (*per me e'arabo*). In a similar vein, the English express bafflement with 'It's all Greek to me', coined by Shakespeare in *Julius Caesar*.

German is unusual in selecting Spanish as its benchmark, in the basic phrase *Das kommt mir spanisch vor* ('That seems Spanish to me'). Ostensibly a curious choice – perhaps there's more at stake here than just linguistic otherness? A clue comes in the fact that Czech has an identical expression (*To je pro mne spanelská vesnice*): Central Europeans' puzzlement at all things Hispanic goes back to the heyday of the Holy Roman Empire.

King Charles I of Spain, a scion of the Habsburg dynasty, was elected Holy Roman Emperor in 1519, taking the title Charles V. The vast and disparate realm he acquired included Austria and Bohemia. Charles was the first Iberian ruler of the Holy Roman Empire, and when he and his entourage ventured east (such as his attendance at the Diet of Augsburg in 1530), the splendour and protocol of his court must have seemed both impressive and profoundly alien to his new subjects.

By the 18th century, the Habsburg (later Austro-Hungarian) Empire controlled most of the same territory once ruled by Charles. Like its predecessor, this state made little political sense, since the interests of its diverse ethnicities were impossible to reconcile. Its dominant culture and language was German, and from this political and administrative élite arose a new equivalent of the 'Spanish' phrase cited above – *das sind mir böhmische Dörfer* ('That's all Bohemian villages to me!'). Its provenance is believed to be German-speaking officials, exasperated at grappling with the consonant-rich names of Czech villages within their bailiwick. Later still, the earlier idiom became conflated with this.

The last word on this fascinating phrase must go to the wonderfully funny and left field German writer of nonsense verse, Christian Morgenstern (1871–1914). Morgenstern riffed on this popular idiom in his poem *Das Böhmische Dorf*, the opening stanzas of which run:

Palmström reist, mit einem Herrn v. Korf,
in ein sogenanntes Böhmisches Dorf.
Unverständlich bleibt ihm alles dort,
von dem ersten bis zum letzten Wort.

...which have been brilliantly translated into English verse, with the appropriate idiom, by Max Knight:

Palmstroem, travelling with a Herr von Korf,
disembarked in Athens at a wharf.
Greek to him was everything he heard,
and he could not understand a word.[1]

---

1 'The Gallows Songs' translated by Max Knight, *Galgenlieder*. Berkeley: University of California Press, 1964.

TO LEAVE IN THE ENGLISH MANNER
(FRENCH)

Filer à l'anglaise – **to slip away unannounced/go AWOL/ take French leave**

A touchstone for the longstanding antagonism between England and France (see **The English have landed**), *filer à l'anglaise* is a rare idiom with a perfect figurative equivalent in the language of the country it seeks to do down. Both it and 'taking French leave' suggest bad manners at best, as in a guest swanning off from a function without bothering to take leave of the host. At worst, they allude to military cowardice; in the French case, this jibe may relate specifically to the tactics employed by Wellington in the Peninsular War, a mixture of hit-and-run guerrilla raids on Napoleon's forces and temporary occupation of fortified towns. This proved extremely successful, but in French eyes merely provided further evidence of perfidious Albion ducking and weaving and refusing to meet their superior troops and commanders head-on in grand, set-piece battles. (Old alliances are revealed by which idiom was chosen for loan-translation: Spain, possibly out of hatred for the French occupation, has *despedirse a la francesa*, whereas Francophile Poland uses *wyjsc po angielsku*.)

But while 'French leave' was in use by the late 18th century, the first examples of *filer à l'anglaise* only appear a century later. And strangely, it seems that it wasn't a conscious riposte to the English phrase but instead had its origins in one of two pieces of French contemporary slang. In the 1890s, the verb *anglaiser* was a colloquial variant of *voler* ('to steal'); hence, to leave in the English manner may have meant 'to slip away like a thief.' The alternative is, at root, even more insulting to the

English. Cadets at the Saint-Cyr military academy (France's Sandhurst) referred to their latrine block as '*l'Anglais*' and so, by extension, *pisser à l'anglaise* became a euphemism for doing a bunk on the pretext of having to answer an urgent call of nature. This was then toned down to the phrase in common usage today. But what a morass of mutual antipathy seethes beneath the surface of these seemingly innocuous coinages!

JIM CROW (US)

Applied to the laws that discriminated against black people in the United States; generalised racism

This loaded expression was the name of either a song or dance associated with the plantations worked by slaves. In 1829 a white performer in Louisville, Kentucky, blackened his face to 'sing Jim Crow' and by the middle of the 19th century such minstrel acts had crossed the Atlantic and were to be seen in the London streets. (Unfortunately, the practice continued: the *Black and White Minstrel Show* was still playing on BBC TV in the 1970s.) After the American Civil War, many southern states enacted statutes which were intended to reinforce separation between blacks and whites, and these swiftly became known as 'Jim Crow laws'. They covered everything from a bar on racial intermarriage to segregation in public places such as restaurants or buses (railroad companies had separate and inferior 'Jim Crow' cars for blacks). In the 20th century, a combination of the civil rights movement, government action and rulings from the US Supreme Court slowly pushed back the Jim Crow laws. The expression 'Jim Crow' is still in frequent use in the sense of 'bigoted' to characterise times and places in which racism was the norm. Martin Luther King remarked that Jim Crow was 'a psychological bird that told him [the white man] that no matter how bad off he was, at least he was a white man, better than the black man.'

NO MOORS ON THE COAST! (Spanish)
No hay Moros en la costa! – **The coast is clear**

Spain's Muslim past as the caliphate of al-Andalus – ruled successively by the Umayyads, the Almoravids and the Almohads – still looms large in its national consciousness. The memory of the Arab conquerors lives on subliminally in phrases like **left under the moon of Valencia** and **not to leave a single puppet with its head on**, and directly in this idiom.

Every year, Spain hosts around 150 separate *Moros y Cristianos* festivals to commemorate the gradual recapture of the country by Christian forces, which was completed by 1492. But this date by no means marked the end of hostilities. Significantly, many of the annual pageants take place along Spain's southern coast, specifically the *Levante español* between the cities of Valencia and Murcia. Long after the *Reconquista*, Barbary corsairs from the ports of Tunis, Tripoli and Algiers continued to plunder this stretch of shore, looting, killing and carrying people off into slavery. Pirate raids remained a persistent problem right up to the late 17th century and beyond.

To try and protect themselves, people living on the Spanish Levant erected a chain of early-warning towers. Solid and made of rough-hewn masonry, these were solely intended as lookout posts, not fortresses. They were manned by sentries who ascended by rope ladders that they pulled up behind them. On sighting approaching Barbary ships, the lookout would yell '*Hay Moros en la costa!*' and signal fires would be lit to warn the inhabitants of towns and villages to flee or take defensive measures.

The negative form of the warning cry then became a common way of indicating that no danger was in the offing.

OPEN THE KIMONO (US)
Reveal what one has, disclose secrets

'Open the kimono' is a business expression and, in keeping with many phrases from the financial/commercial world, it is both colourful and slightly odd. In the Microsoft lexicon, a compendium of phrases widely used at the company, 'open the kimono', although not originating with Microsoft, is explained as 'a somewhat sexist synonym for "open the books" [which] means to reveal the inner workings of a project or company to a prospective new partner'. Since kimonos may be worn by men as well as women, there have been attempts to remove the salacious overtones of the phrase by claiming that 'opening the kimono' is the equivalent of rolling up one's sleeves and getting down to business. An alternative explanation derives from the world of the samurai: to encourage trust, one opens the kimono to reveal not one's undergarments but the fact that one is not carrying any concealed weapons. The most direct origin, and one that retains a commercial aspect, is that it simply describes the teasing behaviour of a geisha or prostitute with her client.

The likelihood is that none of these is true and that the expression never came from Japan in the first place. Rather, it is a faintly mocking American creation, dating from the upsurge in Japanese foreign investment which began in the late 1970s. Japanese partnerships and acquisitions in the United States, the wartime foe and postwar occupier, might well have stirred up ambivalent feelings, ones reflected in a host-country phrase such as 'open the kimono', combining as it does mild traces of racism and sexism and a generally patronising attitude. The phrase can also be used adjectivally in the sense that an organisation might operate an 'open-kimono' policy.

AN ENGLISH WEEK (GERMAN)

Eine englische Woche – [in football or other sports] a week packed with fixtures

In international football, the Germans may have bested England in almost every match that mattered since Wembley in 1966, but at least this idiom suggests some sympathy for our plight. An 'English week' denotes an eight-day period (Saturday to Saturday) in which a club is required to play three games. The English season is particularly packed since, not only are there 20 teams in the Premier League, as opposed to 18 in the *Bundesliga* (meaning four more regular league matches a season), but two-leg fixtures in knockout competitions like the FA and League Cups also have to be fitted in somehow. Add in European commitments such as the Champions or Europa Leagues, and the calendar's getting really crammed.

So, then, this busy schedule might account for the jaded and below-par state of England's top-flight players when, in the summer months, they are called upon to contest international tournaments. Suddenly, the tattooed and pomaded coxcombs who do the business week-in, week-out for their clubs have grown two left feet, and early exits ensue. How sporting of the Germans, though, to provide such a charitable excuse for our national side's serial underachievement.

HEAD HONCHO (US)

Boss/manager

'Honcho' derives from hancho, a word meaning 'squad leader' in Japanese (a han-cho was a corporal or sergeant). It was brought back to the United States by the occupying forces after the Second World War. The word was once sufficient unto itself but it is now usually coupled with 'head', to describe the top person in a company etc. This has the virtue of being alliterative but does not otherwise make much sense since it is the equivalent of saying 'head boss'. The popularity of 'head honcho' both in British and American English may be related to a false etymology. With its echoes of 'hombre' and 'poncho', the phrase looks and sounds Spanish/Mexican and at least one advertisement exists of the 'head honcho' concept illustrated with a figure wearing a sombrero. If this sham Spanish is the explanation for the widespread use of the phrase, then it may be that the users are looking for a testosterone top-up from that language, which also supplies the English language with words like *macho* and *cojones*. As an idiomatic term for the top individual in an organisation, 'head honcho' joins other expressions which combine a hint of mockery with approval: 'big cheese', 'kingpin', 'supremo', 'major leaguer'.

A FRENCH COMPLIMENT (DUTCH)

Een Frans compliment – **empty flattery/an insincere compliment**

Anyone with friends, acquaintances or colleagues from the Netherlands can attest to the fact that they take great pride in speaking as they find. Blunt, direct, frank, to the point: the Dutch wear these terms as badges of honour for their national character and their language. All satire aside, it's a genuine cultural difference that can be the cause of much friction when Anglo-Saxons or others misconstrue it as calculated rudeness. *Onverbloemd* (literally 'unflowered') is the adjective that best encapsulates this trait; ironically for a country boasting thousands of hectares of tulips, lilies, alstroemeria, gerbera and so on, the Dutch decidedly don't say it with flowers.

Conversely, wheedling insincerity is the preserve of foreigners, specifically the mendacious French. With people whose natural mode of discourse isn't the unvarnished truth, you don't know where you are, so a 'French compliment' leaves you unsure whether you've just been praised, or subtly insulted. Most unsettling. The same idea is also expressed in the phrase *Daar is geen word Frans bij* ('There's not a word of French in it'). In other words: 'God's honest truth', 'That's telling it like it is'.

DISSING THE DUTCH

Several idioms bear witness to the great animosity once felt towards the Dutch in England. After winning independence from Spain in the late 16th century, the Dutch Republic adopted a policy of commercial and colonial expansion that set it on an inevitable collision course with its equally ambitious seafaring neighbour across the North Sea. In the 17th century, three brief naval wars were fought between the nations – in 1652–54, 1665–67 and 1672–74 – during the second of which the Dutch launched a daring raid on the fleet anchored at Chatham on the River Medway and inflicted the ultimate humiliation on the English by seizing the Royal Navy's flagship.

But before long the tables were turned. Over the following century, Britain steadily gobbled up the Netherlands' seaborne trading empire and trounced the Dutch in another naval conflict in 1780–84. The British also did their utmost to do down their adversaries in a series of disparaging terms that kept on being added to long after the rivalry had been settled in Britain's favour. Many of them are still in everyday use:

- **Dutch auction:** An auction at which the price steadily drops until a buyer is found.

- **Dutch courage:** Bravery that comes from the consumption of alcohol.

- **Dutch treat/going Dutch:** An entertainment where each person pays for him- or herself.

- **Dutch uncle:** A person whose constant mode is criticism and reproach.

The message couldn't be clearer: perceived Dutch traits of meanness, dourness and so on taint or skew any concept, however positive. Other anti-Dutch coinages that once enjoyed wide currency but have since fallen into disuse are in much the same vein: Dutch widow (a prostitute); Dutch feast (a banquet where the host gets bladdered before the guests); Dutch concert (a hideous cacophony); Dutch gold (bogus gold, an alloy of copper and zinc); and Dutch nightingale (a frog). A general pattern becomes clear: ersatz, shoddy, risible.

And then, of course, there's the ultimate linguistic jibe: 'Double Dutch'. As Bill Bryson explains in his hilarious travel book *Neither Here Nor There*: '…the language sounds like nothing so much as a peculiar version of English.' Little Englanders may not choose to acknowledge it, but German, Dutch and English all perch close together on the Germanic branch of the Indo-European tree. So, this contemptuous dismissal of Dutch as unintelligible gobbledegook must owe more to politically motivated xenophobia than a fair appraisal of the actual difficulty of the language.

The Dutch have, over time, neatly turned the tables by mastering ludicrously colloquial English and answering you in it if you should ever be so rash as to address them in their own language. Touché! Conversely, the English have got off lightly in Dutch. Two common idioms are the opaque *Een Engelse Brief schrijven* (Lit. 'To write an English letter'= to take an afternoon nap) which appears to be having a dig at English indolence, and the crystal-clear *Dat is Engels gaar* (Lit. 'That's done in the English way'= it's not properly cooked) which shies at the age-old Aunt Sally of unpalatable English food.

Chapter 9

WORLD OF WONDER

It's a cruel irony that the effects of global warming will eventually bring us full circle in our relationship to nature. So much for progress. *Homo sapiens* began with an irrational terror of natural phenomena, be they atmospheric (thunder, lightning), geological (earthquakes, volcanic eruptions, tsunamis) or celestial (eclipses, comets). With our growing understanding and exploitation of our surroundings, this primal fear gave way to a frisson of horror when confronted with the nature's sublime grandeur – yet always experienced at one remove, that is, purely on an aesthetic level – in the concept that the 18th century called 'the picturesque'. Now, as our reckless despoliation of the environment creates ever more extreme weather events, we will be plunged back into a state of fear once more. Only this time with good cause.

But before we all go to Hell in a handbasket, here are some idioms relating (ostensibly or actually) to the natural world to muse on.

STEAL SOMEONE'S THUNDER (UK)

To upstage somebody/take credit that is due to someone else

A betting man might stake his all on this idiom originating in some mythological tale or other, in which an angry deity exacts an awful revenge on an upstart god for daring to filch one of the key tools of his celestial trade. Think Prometheus, chained to a rock and having his liver pecked out by birds for stealing fire from the gods. But in this case, the gambler would lose his shirt. For the phrase comes not from mythology, but from the equally cruel and capricious world of the theatre. It has to do with stage thunder.

Stage machinery to help the audience suspend disbelief began with the Ancient Greeks, with their invention of the *deus ex machina*, a god lowered from above to resolve the action and precipitate the denouement of the play. From the Renaissance onwards, the mechanical devices employed to create the illusion of the forces of nature became ever more numerous and elaborate. In Ravenna, Italy, the architect Nicola Sabbatini (1574–1654) published a seminal work with the title *Pratica di fabricar scene e macchine ne' teatri* ('Manual for Constructing Theatrical Scenes and Machines') in 1638. Sabbatini's method for creating thunder consisted of a case of wooden stairs suspended over the stage into which several stone or iron balls, each weighing some 30 pounds, were released. As they rolled down the stepped channel, they produced a sound like thunder.

Thespians are nervous, superstitious creatures at the best of times; concentrating on delivering your lines while cannon-balls careened about above your head can't have been easy. And so safer solutions were sought. At the magnificent Drottningholm Palace Theatre in Stockholm, built in the 1760s, the stage machinery, designed by Donato Stopani, included trapdoors, moving waves, cloud cars and devices for reproducing wind and thunder. Stopani's thunder machine, again located above the stage but now supported on sturdy rafters, was comprised of a box filled with stones suspended from a block and tackle and pivoted around a fulcrum placed at its midpoint. The stones made their ominous rumbling noise by rolling from one end of the box to the other. Other baroque thunder devices, installed in France (at the court theatre at Versailles), Italy and Russia, used a variety of methods to propel a cogged wheel across a resonating wooden platform.

And so to the direct source of the idiom. In 1709, a critic and dramatist manqué called John Dennis (1657–1734) premiered one of his plays, *Appius and Virginia*, at the Drury Lane Theatre in London. Like almost all of Dennis's literary output, this tragedy was a flop and quickly closed. His contemporary, Alexander Pope, then rubbed salt into the wound by mocking the drama in his *Essay on Criticism*, which began an acrimonious and long-running feud between the two men. *Appius and Virginia* would doubtless have long since sunk into total obscurity but for Pope's jibe and for an anecdote told by another contemporary (and a fellow victim of Pope's rapier wit), the actor and playwright Colley Cibber. In his *Lives of the Poets* (1753), Cibber recounted how Dennis returned to Drury Lane, shortly after the failure of his play, to attend a performance of *Macbeth*. Dennis had been proud not only of his written work but also of a new thunder machine (sadly, no details of the construction survive) he had devised specifically for use during *Appius*. So he was outraged to find that the same theatre management that had pulled the plug so unceremoniously on his play was now reusing his stage machinery for *Macbeth*. His words are variously reported, but in one version run: 'That is my thunder, by God! The villains will play my thunder, but not my play!'

Because the origin of this idiom is so relatively recent and culture-specific, it comes as no surprise to learn that there are no direct equivalents in other languages. In sum, a rare example of an undisputed genesis of a common phrase, and a quirky one at that.

SPEAK THROUGH THE FLOWER (GERMAN)

Durch die Blume sprechen – **to hint at/intimate something**

As Geoffrey Grigson's marvellous book *The Englishman's Flora* (1958) explains, flowers were once endowed with the most complex symbolic associations. People in medieval times looking at, say, a piece of stained glass showing a Madonna lily or Albrecht Dürer's *Self-portrait with Eryngium Flower* (1493) would have instantly recognised these blooms as signifying, respectively, purity and conjugal fidelity (Eryngium, the sea holly, also has aphrodisiac connotations). It may well be, then, that the idea of 'speaking through the flower' comes from this lost symbolic mode of expression.

But the more traceable origin of the term is already itself a metaphor: the *flosculus*, or 'little flower' of Latin rhetoric – an ornamental flourish used by an orator to broach a subject indirectly. This device was the stock-in-trade of the medieval Minnesinger, with their deeply allusive language of courtly love: Middle High German referred to it as the *Redebluome*.

By extension, to say something straight out, minus the perfumed veil of the *flosculus*, is rendered in German by the adjective/adverb *unverblümt*, and in Dutch by *onverbloemd* (see **A French compliment**).

SPEND A WHITE NIGHT (FRENCH)

Passer une nuit blanche – **to have a sleepless night/pull an all-nighter**

The older meaning of this idiom is to spend a sleepless night involuntarily, as a result of insomnia. It is used in this sense by Rudyard Kipling in the title of a poem (*La Nuit*

Blanche) of 1887, which describes the sleeplessness of a heavy drinker suffering from the DTs. Kipling prefaces the poem with a playful disclaimer, teasing readers who might try to interpret the work as the fruit of his personal experience.

The ultimate origin of the phrase is unknown, though one suggestion is that it may relate to the medieval practice of knightly investiture, for which candidates would keep a vigil throughout the preceding night, dressed all in white, as a sign of purity. The one problem here (incidentally, the phrase also exists in Italian, as *passare una notte in bianco*) is that this is clearly a voluntary night without sleep – which brings us on to the idiom's second meaning.

Today, a far more common usage of *une nuit blanche* is for an all-night summer arts festival. The concept was pioneered in the Breton city of Nantes in the late 1980s, later spreading to Paris and then further afield, to Montréal and Toronto. European cities such as Rome, Brussels, Paris, Madrid and Bucharest now coordinate their festivals as '*Nuits Blanches Europe*'. The idea of an all-night cultural shindig has since been embraced by Britain's capital of cool, Brighton, which held its first White Night/Nuit Blanche in 2008.

The white night has also become a firm fixture in Tel Aviv, where it is known as *Layla Lavan*. But perhaps the most appropriate place, idiomatically speaking, for the phenomenon to have taken root is St Petersburg; located at a latitude of 59° 55' N, the White Nights here (inaugurated in 1993, and held in June) are literally that, with darkness largely banished by the midnight sun around the summer solstice.

TALL POPPY SYNDROME (Australian)

Envy of those who are more successful, talented etc., coupled with the desire to see them lose their status

The roots of this saying seem to go back thousands of years to the legend of Tarquin, king of Rome, who when asked what should be done with the occupants of a neighbouring and hostile city, replied not with words but by going out to his garden and striking the heads off the tallest poppies. His silent message was that the most prominent citizens of that city should be disposed of. The desire to cut down metaphorical tall poppies first emerges in print in the middle of the 19th century, and if it is not suggested by ancient legend, its source is presumably the height and distinctive colour of the flowers in, say, a field of corn.

If the wish is expressed by the ordinary person, it may seem no more than the product of envy or spite. When voiced by a politician, it can become part of an egalitarian programme of levelling, as it was for the premier of New South Wales in 1931, who explicitly stated his policy to be one of 'cutting the heads off tall poppies'. It was characteristic of Margaret Thatcher that, in a speech given in New York in 1975 before she was elected Prime Minister, she should reverse the levelling message: 'I believe you have a saying in the Middle West: "Don't cut down the tall poppies. Let them rather grow tall." I would say, let our children grow tall and some taller than others if they have the ability in them to do so.' The difference between the politicians as well as the places where these comments were made is significant. 'Tall poppy syndrome' has always grown readily in Australia, where it seems to have originated, and in most other English-speaking countries with the apparent exception of the United States, where achievement and talent are praised rather than denigrated. At least, that's their story. In the early 1980s, the wish to cut down 'tall poppies' turned into a syndrome, which was a popular tag at the time (the China Syndrome, Stockholm syndrome), with an underlying hint that there was something a bit unhealthy about the wish to see others cut down to size.

A REED-TRUTH (GERMAN)

eine Binsenwahrheit – **a truism/commonplace**

Botanically, there's nothing straighter and simpler than the leaves of plants of the family *Juncaceae* – wetland reeds or rushes. It's this quality of plainness to which the German idiom *eine Binsenwahrheit* most probably alludes (much like the English term 'platitude'). It may ultimately have its origin in the Latin saying *nodum in scirpo quaerere* – 'to search for knots on a rush', i.e. to look for complications where there are none.

An alternative etymology concerns the sound of reeds rather than their appearance. A Greek legend tells how Midas (king of Phrygia and he of the golden touch) once disputed Apollo's victory over Pan in a musical contest. To punish him for having such undiscriminating hearing, Apollo transformed his ears into those of a donkey. Mortified, Midas took to wearing a turban to hide his hairy new appendages, but inevitably his barber found out while cutting his hair. The king swore him to secrecy, but hairdressers are a garrulous bunch, and the man eventually felt compelled to divulge what he knew. Digging a deep hole in the ground, he whispered his secret into it before shovelling back the soil. But a thick bed of reeds grew over the spot and betrayed what the earth had been told in confidence, whispering: 'Midas has asses' ears'. And so *eine Binsenwahrheit* came to mean a piece of common knowledge, an open secret.

Curiously, another German idiom involving reeds hints at pretty much the opposite situation, i.e. concealment and obscurity. Deriving from duck hunting, *In die Binsen gehen* literally refers to the quarry taking refuge in a reed bed, never to be flushed out, and metaphorically means 'to go down the drain/come to nothing'. In describing a lost opportunity, it has an affinity to the modern English political cliché 'kicking something [e.g. an idea or proposal] into the long grass'.

ON CLOUD NINE (UK)
Very happy/in an elated state

There is a disputed explanation for this phrase (which dates from the 1960s), a derivation from the system of cloud classification used by the US Weather Bureau. According to this theory, 'cloud nine' describes a particularly high and fluffy type or – to speak scientifically – cumulonimbus. One of the problems with this explanation is that it is almost too precise, while another is that there are more than nine cloud divisions. It seems more likely that the expression results from the confluence of several different ideas relating both to height and to a state of euphoria.

The metaphorical link between clouds and dreaminess or absent-mindedness goes back a long way, evident in phrases such as 'head in the clouds' or 'cloud cuckoo land'. There is also the suggestion of self-absorption, of wanting to be left alone in a state of splendid isolation. Early in their 50-year career, *Get off of My Cloud* was the Rolling Stones' follow-up single to the phenomenal success of *Satisfaction*. Then there is the question of altitude, metaphorically speaking. Being 'high', in the colloquial sense of being intoxicated, is found as early as the 17th century although the word does not really come into its own until the 20th century, when its application is more often to the effects of drugs rather than drink. An older variant equates cloud eight with drunkenness, so the inflationary process which is often found in language may have propelled us higher to cloud nine. Since it describes a more than pleasant state, there may also be a glance at the usually positive associations of the number nine, which like three and five has often been considered to have mystical significance.

DRAW UP PLANS ON THE COMET (French)

Tirer les plans sur la comète – **to build castles in the air/make unrealistic plans**

In a time before accurate astronomical observation, people were terrified of comets. Whereas most other celestial bodies appeared or disappeared with reassuring regularity, comets were unpredictable and ephemeral, trailing their fiery tails across the sky and then vanishing. As a result, they were commonly seen as harbingers of doom, messages from an angry god venting his wrath on dissolute humankind. Samuel Pepys' Diary entry of 17 August 1665 mentions 'a new comet which is said to have lately shone', and the plague that began to ravage London immediately afterwards was attributed in popular superstition to its appearance. Even as late as 1910, when Earth passed through the tail of Halley's Comet, scaremongers put it about that every living being would be asphyxiated by the cyanogen gas it contained (the gas is present, but is so diffuse as to be entirely harmless).

This seeming randomness in when and where comets would appear (Pepys never did get to see the 1665 event) meant that anyone basing their plans on a sighting would be indulging in a highly speculative and risky venture. The French idiom, then, is a deliberate oxymoron, linking the suggestion of foreknowledge and certainty implicit in all worthwhile planning with something inherently unreliable and fleeting.

'Drawing up plans on the comet' took on a whole new sinister dimension in 1997. We have already had cause (see **Drink the Kool-Aid**) to note the propensity of religious cults for grotesque acts of self-destruction: in this instance, the appearance of a comet was the catalyst of another mass suicide. On 26 March 1997 in California, cult leader Marshall Herff Applewhite and 39 of his acolytes in the 'Heaven's Gate' group killed themselves with a mixture of barbiturates and vodka. The reason? Applewhite claimed that the Comet Hale-Bopp, which from Earth was visible to the naked eye for 18 months from May 1996 onwards, was trailing in its wake an alien spacecraft, to which they would all be teleported once they'd terminated their temporal existence.

'FOR THE RAIN IT RAINETH EVERY DAY'

Of all the weather features followed eagerly by those who live in temperate parts of the world, perhaps none is regarded with such ambivalent feelings as rain. Feste the clown's wry song at the end of Shakespeare's *Twelfth Night* acknowledges that whatever else happens in the world, there's one thing you can count on: the rain that descends every day. Not surprisingly, it is at the root of quite a few regular expressions, such as 'taking a rain check', a US idiom signifying a promise to fulfil an obligation at a later date. This long-established phrase originated in the sports world, when a spectator at an outdoor event which was cancelled because of bad weather would be given a rain check (ticket) guaranteeing free admission to a forthcoming game. At some point in the early 20th century, the phrase acquired a metaphorical sense and became more about the recipient's response to an invitation than about the offering of a free ticket. Not quite a yes, not quite a no, 'taking a rain check' allows the speaker to escape the embarrassment of turning down an offer by deferring acceptance to an unspecified future date. Rain is also given a welcome in an expression such as 'rainmaker', originally a tribal figure credited with the magical ability to cause the rain to fall, but now applied to a successful individual, often in a law firm, who brings in business by attracting new clients or generating income. The negative side of the subject is shown in expressions such as 'putting something aside for a rainy day' or the comment about 'not wanting to rain on someone's parade', signifying a reluctance to spoil someone's enjoyment, often by raising objections to a plan, delivering unwelcome news and so on. A later US variant is 'pissing on someone's parade.'

Chapter 10

MATTERS SPIRITUAL

Every year, British newspapers (and, for that matter, some foreign ones too) report on the new headwords that have made it into the latest update of the *Oxford English Dictionary*. This is newsworthy because new words are seen as registering the concerns of the age – say, our obsession with new technology and media (e.g. *tweeting, podcast, Lol-speak*), a perceived decline in moral standards (*date-rape drug, waterboarding*) or vacuous celebrity culture (*WAG, bling, A-lister*).

As with neologisms, so with idioms. Though less obvious as touchstones of current trends than new coinages, they can still reflect prevailing attitudes. As you'd expect, most of the phrases in this chapter come from the Bible or from Europe's long centuries of religious observance and religious conflict. But significantly, if we think of more recent idioms on a religious theme, a common denominator emerges: mockery. Think of the exasperated exclamation 'Christ on a bike!', or that seemingly ubiquitous ironic rhetorical question: 'Is the Pope a Catholic?' (made facetious by its spoken or unspoken coda 'Do bears shit in the woods?'). These aren't discussed here – not much to say about them, in truth – but one that is discussed is an old Spanish idiom given a modern twist: 'Where Christ lost his lighter.'

All very amusing, but also very irreverent. What Godless times we live in. *O tempora, o mores!*

THE CHERETHITES AND THE PELETHITES
(GERMAN)

Krethi und Plethi – **every Tom, Dick, and Harry/hoi polloi**

In the Old Testament, 8:18 of the Second Book of Samuel begins: 'And Benaiah the son of Jehoaida was over both the Cherethites and the Pelethites.' Other passages from the books of this prophet and from that of Ezekiel, which mention the two groups separately, identify them broadly as a group of elite mercenaries in the service of King David.

Scholars have argued over whether the two groups were actually different from, or synonymous with, one another (being either all Philistines, or possibly Cretans). Certainly, the Books of Samuel identify them both as coming from a site called Ziklag in the Negev Desert; they may denote successive waves of Cretan migration to the area. Aramaic and Syriac translations of the Hebrew Bible render the phrase as 'bowmen and slingers' or 'executioners and messengers'; modern authorities largely reject these interpretations.

But these niceties of Biblical scholarship needn't concern us here. The German phrase *Krethi und Plethi*, which first appears in Martin Luther's Bible of 1534, soon became a disparaging term for an assorted rabble. The disparaging tone implicit in the usage is no doubt traceable to the fact that these groups were soldiers of fortune, who have always been feared and despised in equal measure.

A similarly pejorative term in German for 'all and sundry' is *Hinz und Kunz*: these are abbreviated forms of the Christian names Heinrich and Konrad, which were extremely common in the Middle Ages. This phrase was turned to ironic advantage in the name chosen for a German street newspaper sold by the homeless, launched in 1993 on the model of *The Big Issue*:

Hinz und Kunzt (the second word a pun on the German word for 'art').

THE WAY OF ST JAMES (Spanish)

El camino de Santiago – the Milky Way

Santiago de Compostela in Galicia, where the remains of St James the Great were reputedly discovered in AD 813, is one of Catholicism's holiest sites. It became a pilgrimage destination from the 10th century onwards, exceeded in pre-eminence only by Rome and Jerusalem. The fervour attached to the legend of the apostle helped this remote northern region of Spain become a centre of resistance to the Moorish conquest of Spain. The *reconquista* found its launch pad here.

The Way of St James, the pilgrimage route that runs from the Pyrenees to Santiago, has long been associated with the Milky Way. One explanation is that pilgrims were guided to the holy site at the ends of the known Earth (Finisterre) by the orientation of this diffuse band of stars in the night sky. Folk etymology has it that the name 'Compostela' literally means 'field of stars', though this is questionable. In any event, the official symbol of the route is a stylised scallop shell (the symbol of St James) set within a field of stars on a blue background.

From an early date, the route was well supplied with hospitals and hospices and, from the 12th century on, Christians came from far and wide to visit Santiago, many doubtless attracted by the prospect of earning an indulgence (a remission of sins) for completing the devotional journey. It was in the medieval period that a legend arose which maintained that the dust kicked up by the thousands of pilgrims beating a path to Galicia was responsible for creating the myriad stars in the Milky Way. This is one of those retrospective explanations, or 'aetiological myths', so familiar to the idiom hunter.

Another such myth is contained in the *Liber Sancti Jacobi* ('Book of St James'), otherwise known as the *Codex Calixtinu*, after Pope Callixtus II (r.1119–24), an avid proponent of the pilgrimage. Book IV of this 12th-century manuscript, which combines homilies and stories from the life of the saint with a practical guide for the traveller, gives an account of the posthumous part played by St James in the Spanish reconquest. The saint is said to have appeared to Charlemagne in a dream and urged him to liberate his tomb from the Moors, showing him the route he should follow by pointing to the Milky Way. This story had clear propagandistic intent, and generated the legend of Santiago Matamoros ('St James the Moor Slayer'). As with so many Spanish idioms (see **No Moors on the coast!; Not leave a single puppet with its head on; Left under the moon of Valencia**), the Moors, those bugbears of Iberian Christendom, also put in a guest appearance here.

TO LIVE LIKE GOD IN FRANCE (GERMAN)

Wie Gott in Frankreich leben – **to live in the lap of luxury/ live high on the hog/live the life of Riley**

The origins of this idiom – which also works in Dutch (*leven als God in Frankrijk*) and Spanish (*vivir como Dios en Francia*) – have been mulled over for centuries, and still excite debate on Internet discussion boards.

Let's begin by clearing out some obvious dross. Some commentators home in on Louis XIV, a monarch who lived in conditions of godlike opulence at Versailles. Yet for all his conspicuous consumption, Louis was still the *Roi Soleil* (not the *Dieu Soleil*). Another suggestion relates to the Avignon papacy (1309–76); but again, these were antipopes residing in southern France and not gods, nor is there any evidence to suggest they lived more lavishly than their Roman rivals.

A marginally more plausible – but ultimately shaky – derivation comes from an anecdote about the 16th-century Holy Roman Emperor Maximilian I (d. 1519), told by an author named Zincgref-Weidner in his *Apophthegmata* (1693). Maximilian supposedly once said in private that if he were a god with two sons, the elder would succeed him as ruling deity of the Empire, while the younger would be King of France. This bit of hubris, though, actually reveals nothing more than the scale of Maximilian's dynastic ambition: to secure Habsburg control over the two great power blocs of Europe at the time. When all's said and done, he only wanted his second son to become the French *king*.

Leapfrogging Avignon, Maximilian and the Sun King, a far more likely explanation is rooted in the French Revolution and its aftermath. The leaders of the revolution espoused reason over Christianity, and the strong anti-clerical dimension of the uprising was driven by the Catholic clergy's closeness to the *ancien régime*. But when they realised that organised religion was key to a stable society, in 1794 the revolutionaries instituted the 'Cult of the Supreme Being'. Pensioned off, and with no worshippers importuning him, the Christian god was free to live a life of ease within the borders of the new France.

Alternatively, *wie Gott* may be a corruption of *wie Goten* – specifically the *Westgoten*, or Visigoths. According to this interpretation, the phrase comes from Spain, where it was used by the native Hispano-Roman population of their erstwhile neighbours and sometime rulers. In the early 5th century, the Visigoths had been rewarded for their support of the moribund Western Roman Empire by being granted effective control of a tract of *Gallia Aquitania* (Aquitaine) by the Emperor Honorius; as *foederati* of Rome, they had opposed hostile encroachments by other Germanic peoples like the Vandals, Alans and Suevi. In Aquitaine, the Visigoths lived well off tax-farming concessions, collecting revenue from local aristocrats. Later, in 454–461 AD, they invaded Spain at Rome's behest, defeating the Suevi and brutally sacking many cities. Over time, they consolidated their grip over southwestern France and the Iberian Peninsula and founded the Visigothic Kingdom, which lasted until the 8th century. During their rule, the Visigoths, who numbered less than two per cent of the kingdom's c.10 million inhabitants, kept themselves separate from the native population. Finally driven out of Spain by the Moorish conquest, many (by now Catholic) Visigoths moved north to the territory of their former enemy, the Franks. By the reign of Charlemagne, many 'naturalised' Visigoths had risen to a position of influence in the Frankish Kingdom. Over three centuries of humiliation, and forced to witness the Visigoths always 'landing on their feet', it is easy to imagine the resentful people of Spain coining this phrase.

BELIEVE YOU'VE SPRUNG FROM THE THIGH OF JUPITER (FRENCH)

Se croire sorti de la cuisse de Jupiter – **to have a very high opinion of yourself/think you're God's gift**

The Greek supreme god Zeus (Roman: Jupiter) was a skirt-chaser on an epic scale. He famously took the form of a swan to seduce Leda and sowed marital discord between Amphitryon and Alcmene, while the four Galilean moons of the planet Jupiter are all named after Jovian conquests (Io, Callisto and Europa were female, and Ganymede was a beautiful boy: the deity swung both ways).

Zeus also had his way with Semele, daughter of King Cadmus of Thebes and his wife Harmonia. When Zeus' jealous spouse Hera learned of the pregnancy, she visited the expectant mother in the guise of her old nurse and craftily sowed sufficient doubt in her mind over the identity of the father that Semele summoned Zeus to appear to settle the matter. Zeus knew this would be the end of her – mortals could not behold the divine countenance and live; he originally came to her in human form. Yet he had made a promise to grant her every wish, and so reluctantly complied. Despite using his smallest thunderbolt to descend to Earth, Zeus could not prevent Semele from being reduced to ashes. But as she was dying, he snatched their unborn son Dionysus (Bacchus) from her womb and quickly sewed him into a gash made in his own thigh to conceal him from Hera. Two months later, the boy-god was born. While he was growing up, Zeus continued to look out for Dionysus, conveying him to places of safety and transforming him into a goat kid in an attempt to escape the wrath of his vengeful wife.

So, to think yourself sprung from the thigh of Jupiter is to believe that you lead a charmed life, basking in the warm sun of divine protection. Of course, because this is mythology, we suspend disbelief at the anatomical impossibility of it all; some commentators, pointing to an epithet of Dionysus – *Enorchos* (i.e. 'in testicles') – suggest that he may even have emerged from Zeus' scrotum. And so it is for a more modern, and infinitely more vulgar, equivalent French phrase for someone who is far too big for his boots: *il pête plus haut que son cul* ('He farts higher than his arse')[1].

WHAT GOES AROUND COMES AROUND (US)
Events, fashions etc. go in a full circle/a good (bad) deed will be rewarded (punished) when the doer finds himself on the receiving end

There are two slightly diverging meanings to this US-based idiom, which emerged some time during the later 20th century but which, as a concept, is surely as old as humankind. The first is a simple observation that there are cycles in everything from business to politics to dress, as in this representative quotation from the *New York Times*: 'Probably the most frequently uttered observation about fashion is that what goes around comes around (and then keeps going, and coming etc.).' In this sense, what goes around comes around – or WGACA – is synonymous with 'going full circle' and carries no moral weight at all. The other sense is an updating of the biblical observation that 'whatsoever a man soweth, that shall he also reap'. This interpretation is also related to the Hindu and Buddhist concept of karma, the hard-to-translate idea that one's destiny is based on one's previous actions, perhaps in an earlier life. There may be a retributive aspect to karma, and there almost always is to 'what goes around comes around' since the comment tends to be applied to examples of bad or vicious behaviour, shameless actions and so on, which come back to haunt the perpetrator in some possibly ironic form. Shakespeare has two versions of

1 The Georges Brassens song *Les funérailles d'antan* includes the phrase *mourir plus haut que leur cul* ('to die above their station').

WGACA, both negative. In *King Lear*, a fatally wounded character says 'the wheel is come full circle', acknowledging the justice of his death and referring to the wheel of fortune. And in *Twelfth Night*, the humilated Malvolio is told 'thus the whirligig of time brings in [its] revenges'. The whirligig – a spinning top or a merry-go-round – foreshadows the inescapable circularity of fate implied by 'what goes around comes around'.

ONE POPE DIES, THEY MAKE ANOTHER
(ITALIAN)

Morto un papa, se ne fa un'altro – **life goes on/there's plenty more fish in the sea**

Protestants and non-believers sometimes make the mistake of assuming that Catholics are universally devout. This may hold good in places remote from the Holy See: it certainly once did for Ireland, and still does for the Philippines. But if this idiom is anything to go by, those at the epicentre of the faith are decidedly blasé about the whole business. Its matter-of-factness hints at the world-weary knowledge that things go on the same, no matter who's at the helm. Unsurprising, really: down the centuries and millennia, Roman Catholics have seen it all and are entitled to feel less than euphoric about change.

Life imitates art, or in this case the artistry of popular parlance. In 1978, the phrase came home to roost more hastily than the Church could have anticipated (discounting crazy conspiracy theories about the event): Pope John Paul I died after a reign of just 33 days, and was succeeded by Pope John Paul II. The king is dead, long live the king...

DON'T GET INVOLVED IN THEOLOGY
(SPANISH)

No te metas en teologías – **Don't meddle in things that don't concern you**

Theology (along with the related discipline of philosophy) stood at the very pinnacle of learning in medieval universities. The 'seven liberal arts' taught there came in two parts: the *trivium*, the three foundation subjects of grammar, logic and rhetoric, which led on to the *quadrivium* (astronomy, music, arithmetic and geometry). These, in turn, were seen as only an anteroom for the study of theology. The disputations on matters of Biblical textual exegesis conducted by such renowned schoolmen of the Middle Ages as Duns Scotus, Thomas Aquinas and William of Ockham thus required great skill in reasoning and years of academic training. By definition, as the Spanish phrase says, theology was something you really ought not to dabble in without the requisite intellectual armoury.

Humility in deferring to another's superior knowledge is now a quaint, outmoded concept: hosts of radio phone-in programmes daily exhort us to offer our two penn'orth on subjects that most of us know absolutely nothing about. In the past, such presumption was rightly lambasted. In 1819, the essayist William Hazlitt coined the marvellous term 'ultracrepidarian' for someone who comments outside his or her area of competence. It derives from a classical allusion. The Latin author Pliny tells the story of a famous 4th-century BC Greek painter, Apelles (a contemporary of Alexander the Great), who used to set up his pictures in public and conceal himself nearby to eavesdrop on the comments of passers-by. On one occasion, he overheard a shoemaker criticising his depiction of a sandal for having one loop too few. Fair enough, the man knew what he was talking about; Apelles duly corrected the error, only to have the shoemaker return and, encouraged by seeing his advice heeded, proceed to carp at the painter's rendition of the subject's leg. This was too much for Apelles, who emerged from his hiding-place to tell the shoemaker 'not to judge beyond his sandals' (*ne supra crepidam judicaret*). Later versions of the same story modified the phrase to the more familiar *ne sutor ultra crepidam* – 'let the shoemaker venture no further', or 'the cobbler should stick to his last'. It's so very tempting to go further and say that the man was clearly talking cobblers, but this of course comes from a completely different source – Cockney rhyming slang ('cobbler's awls' = balls).

Bringing this full circle, another way of telling someone in Spanish to mind their own business is a direct translation of the Latin injunction: *Zapatero a tus zapatos!* (literally, 'Shoemaker, to your shoes!').

READ TO SOMEONE FROM THE BOOK OF LEVITICUS (German)

Jemandem die Leviten lesen – **to read someone the riot act**

The Third Book of Moses (i.e. of the Old Testament, or the Hebrew Bible) largely comprises rules of conduct for priests. The Levites, descendants of the Tribe of Levi, were originally assigned the role of assistants to priests (*Kohanim*) in the sanctuary, but the term gradually became synonymous with 'priest'; hence the more familiar title of the Biblical book: Leviticus.

In the Middle Ages, it was customary for passages from Leviticus to be read out in Benedictine monasteries during acts of devotion and penitence, followed by sermons admonishing members of the order to keep their godly calling firmly in mind. The overall effect was that of a harangue, and so the concept embedded itself as a colourful circumlocution for a good dressing-down.

The English figurative phrase 'to read someone the riot act' derives from the practice of reading out sections of the Draconian law of that name to unlawful and potentially unruly assemblies. It was passed by the British government in 1714 to try and quell Jacobite unrest. The act made it a felony for a group of 12 or more to refuse to disperse after hearing the proclamation. Punishments included a term of imprisonment with hard labour, transportation and even the death penalty. After falling into disuse from the mid-19th century on, the Riot Act was finally repealed in 1967.

MOJO (US)
Influence/power/charm

In the early part of the 20th century in the United States, the move northwards of large numbers of black workers looking for new opportunities in the cities – as well as escaping restrictive racial laws in the southern states – led to a resurgence of black culture which became known as the 'Harlem Renaissance'. Some African-Americans wanted to discard their distinctive idiom and adopt the style of the white mainstream, while others saw it as perfectly valid. It is ironic that their slang terms – many of them dating from the 1920s and some from earlier (jive, chick, hype, jam, mellow, pad) – were eagerly taken up by white speakers who wanted to be seen as 'cool', another quintessential black expression.

Among these terms is 'mojo', which, like the associated term 'voodoo' probably originated in west Africa, and denoted magic powers or the talisman which is needed to invoke them. The word has turned into a catch-all expression because the definition of 'mojo' has moved away from its quasi-religious origins to become so fluid that it can apply to almost anything. Frequently spoken of as something which is lost or perhaps got back, 'mojo' is synonymous with a variety of desirable attributes: charisma, sexiness, sense of purpose, self-assurance, influence. One of the best descriptions comes from journalist Barbara Ellen, who describes it in the *Observer* as 'the "stuff" inside a person that gives them that extra bit of fizz and sparkle and swagger to get through life. Other ways of describing "mojo" would be "soul" or "chutzpah". And it's important, this mojo thing, because it gives a person a subtle but exhilarating sense of confidence and momentum.'

WHERE CHRIST GAVE THE THREE VOICES
(SPANISH)

Donde Cristo dio las tres voces – **in the back of beyond/ the middle of nowhere**

The allusion in this idiom for somewhere impossibly remote (of which there are plenty in Spain) is opaque, but is likely to be to the Temptation of Christ. As described in the Synoptic Gospels (Matthew, Mark and Luke), after being baptised, Jesus spent 40 days fasting in the wilderness, during which time he was tempted three times by the Devil. Admittedly, the formulation '*gave* the three voices' is puzzling; perhaps we're to construe it as an unfinished phrase, filling in the implied blank with something like 'the brush-off', 'short shrift', 'the cold shoulder'. After all, anyone who knows their Scripture will be familiar with Christ's dismissal of his tormentor: 'Get thee behind me, Satan' (Luke 4:1).

In this circumlocution for a forgotten, desolate place, there's a faint echo of *Cristo si è fermato a Eboli* ('Christ Stopped at Eboli'), Italian author Carlo Levi's 1945 memoir of his internal exile under Mussolini's fascist regime to Basilicata, deep in the south on the 'arch' of Italy's boot-shaped peninsula. The inhabitants of this region used the phrase that gave the book its title to suggest that they were so far off the beaten track that even Christianity had passed them by.

One of the many marvellous things about idioms is their ability to evolve, and with the passage of time (not unlike **To know more than Lepe**) this phrase gave rise to a number of increasingly irreverent spin-offs. These usually take the form of variations on *Donde Cristo perdió...* ('Where Christ lost...') and include such items as *el gorro* (his cap), *los clavos* (his nails, i.e. from the Cross, not his fingernails), and *las alpagatas* (his espadrilles). But the best, and most recent, variant of all is undoubtedly *Donde Cristo perdió el mechero* – 'Where Christ lost his (cigarette) lighter'. To the irreligious, the image of Jesus, fag in mouth, tetchily searching the undergrowth for his missing Zippo, is delightfully absurd.

ST NEVER'S DAY (GERMAN)

Sankt Nimmerleinstag – **never in a month of Sundays**

In German, a playful way of expressing the notion that something is highly unlikely ever to come about is to refer to the fictitious 'St Never's Day' (with *nimmer* meaning 'never' and *-lein* a diminutive suffix appended just for rhetorical effect). Fixing a deadline not by the calendrical date but by the saint's day associated with it was widespread legal practice in German-speaking lands from the early Middle Ages onwards. For instance, the date on which agreements lapsed or servants' employment was terminated would often be set on the feast day of a major saint, such as St John the Baptist (24 June).

There used to be some more scurrilous variations on this theme: *Fest der Beschneidung Mariä* ('Feast of the Blessed Virgin Mary's Circumcision') and *Des Teufels Himmelfahrttag* ('Devil's Ascension Day'; by analogy with *Christi Himmelfahrt*, the German term for the Ascension). The latter crops up in the writings of Martin Luther and both appear to have their roots in Catholic-baiting, by lampooning Rome's obsession with saints' days and other religious beanfeasts.

In 1943, the dramatist Bertolt Brecht made telling use of *Sankt Nimmerleinstag* in his play *The Good Person of Szechwan*. At the end of an abortive wedding ceremony, the bridegroom launches into 'The Ballad of Saint Never's Day' to express his bitter disappointment at not receiving the dowry he expected. Its ironic refrain runs:

> *On Saint Never's Day*
> *There will be Paradise on Earth.*

An exact French equivalent, likewise employing a spurious saint's day, is the idiom *à la Saint Glinglin*. This too originates in the medieval farming cycle, when peasants were required to discharge their debts on the first major feast day following their receipt of income from the harvest. Saint Glinglin developed as a joking reference to evasion of this unwelcome obligation, and alludes onomatopoeically to the trumpets that will sound on Judgement Day (*glinger* being an archaic equivalent of modern French *sonner*). French also adopted the phrase *aux calendes grecques* from the Latin *ad kalendas graecas* ('On the Greek Calends'). This circumlocution for 'never' played on the knowledge that the Calends, the first day of each month, was peculiar to the Roman calendar. In his *Lives of the Twelve Caesars*, the Roman historian Suetonius attributes the phrase to the emperor Augustus, who was wont to use it to bemoan the fact that bad debtors endlessly delayed settling up with him.

BIBLICAL IDIOMS

The King James version of the Bible – so called because it was translated by a group set up by King James I (1566–1625) – has been replaced by more up-to-date translations such as the New English Bible (1970), but whenever a comparison is required for a new translation, it is almost always the King James version which is cited as the template, for its musicality, its dignity and grace. Still part of the fabric of the English language, the King James Bible has for centuries provided us with a large number of everyday expressions such as 'fly in the ointment', 'by the skin of one's teeth', 'thorn in the flesh', 'salt of the earth' and 'labour of love'. Slightly less familiar may be some of the names of Biblical characters who have come to stand for some quality that they embodied.

- *Jezebel*: The wife of King Ahab of Israel who introduced the worship of pagan gods and who was denounced by the prophet Elijah. From a patriarchal point of view, a shameless woman – and one who wears too much make-up. Curiously, 'jezebel' was also 19th-century slang for penis.

- *Jonah:* Someone whose presence brings bad luck. Jonah, a prophet in the Old Testament, was thrown overboard by the sailors on a ship because they believed he had brought down a storm on their heads. Swallowed by a fish or a whale, he was regurgitated three days later.

- *Judas:* A traitor. From Judas Iscariot, the disciple who betrayed Christ for 30 pieces of silver. A byword for treachery, he hanged himself (by tradition, from the Judas tree). He also gives his name to the Judas hole/window (a spy-hole in a door) and a Judas kiss (an act or gesture which is deceptively affectionate).

- *Job:* A person who is long-suffering. God permitted Job to be afflicted with various misfortunes to test his patience. A Job's comforter is someone who offers sympathy but makes things worse by the way he or she tries to console the sufferer.

Chapter 11

HUMAN FLESH

At first sight, this is unpromising terrain for the idiom collector. Phrases involving parts of the body are generally as straightforward in their meaning as *tamata* – those little metal plaques left as votive offerings in Greek Orthodox churches, depicting the limb or organ that the supplicant wants to be healed. Or, if you prefer, as plain as the nose on your face. As such, there's really not much to say about 'toe the line', 'give someone the elbow', 'bring something to its knees' and so on, or their foreign equivalents.

Even so, we believe we've unearthed a few good ones here, intriguing enough to catch your eye.

DRAW THE ARSE CARD (German)

Die Arschkarte ziehen – **to draw the short straw/get a bum deal**

Like **An English week**, this is an idiom from the world of football, that sport which the Germans play so maddeningly well.

It only comes from sometime after 1970, the date when referees started issuing red or yellow cards to players who committed fouls. They were introduced at the World Cup finals that year in Mexico, following confusion over the dismissal of a player in the England v. Argentina quarter-final at Wembley in 1966. To avoid pulling out the wrong card, refs tended to keep the yellow one, for bookings, in their shirt breast pocket, and the red, for sendings-off, in the back pocket of their shorts.

It's rare for a player not to feel aggrieved at being told to take an early bath, however blatantly he may have scythed down an opponent. And so the idiom entered popular parlance to signal, in any context, a feeling of being hard done by. A feeling, by the by, that we feel should be wholly unfamiliar to the German national side, given the number of controversial refereeing decisions that have gone their way since 1966.

NOT TO HAVE TWO FINGERS OF FOREHEAD
(Spanish)

No tener dos dedos de frente – **to be as thick as two short planks/not the sharpest tool in the box**

People can be very literal-minded. Take, for example, the image of the big, bald chrome-dome: we automatically assume that it houses a huge brain, with an intellectual capacity to match. Most famously, the arch-villain of the *Dan Dare* comic strip of the 1950s, the Mekon, was an alien with a weedy body and a massive cranium. And the term 'egghead' is commonly used by the tabloids to describe someone even vaguely highbrow or intelligent.

In fact, there's no correlation whatsoever between cranial size and intellectual capacity (or even brain size and intellectual capacity, for that matter). The assumption that there is is born of a long history of pseudoscience, beginning with the discipline of phrenology (or 'cranioscopy'), developed in around 1800 by the German physiologist Franz Joseph Gall. Phrenology posited a direct link between the shape of a person's skull and the degree of advancement of their mental faculties. In the late 19th century, this anthropometric approach found practical application in Italian criminologist Cesare Lombroso's theory of inherited criminality. 'Born criminals', claimed Lombroso, could be identified by such physical attributes as abnormally long arms, large ears, and a sloping forehead. These features, reminiscent as they were of early hominids, showed criminals to be a primitive or subhuman form of man.

In this same vein, the Spanish idiom stigmatises a forehead that begins to recede from just two fingers' width above the brow ridge as the mark of a halfwit. No matter that scientists have long since discovered that Neanderthals weren't the dullards of popular myth but in all probability were every bit as smart as we are. Old prejudices die hard.

HOOKER (US)

A prostitute

Fighting Joe Hooker served in the Potomac region as a Union general in the American Civil War, although his 'Fighting' nickname was apparently the result of a newspaper error when a punctuating dash disappeared from a headline. Hooker had a reputation as a hard drinker and womaniser, and army headquarters were said by a disapproving observer to resemble 'a combination of barroom and brothel'. It's reasonable to conclude therefore that 'hooker' – arguably the most common US slang term for a prostitute – should have originated with Fighting Joe. But there are references to hookers which pre-date the general's career and a more likely source for the word is an area on the south-east of the New York waterfront once known as 'Corlear's Hook' after a Dutch settler. It was a noted red-light district. But the term may have been in existence before becoming, as it were, hooked up with a bit of Manhattan since hookers have never had a good name, whatever their trade. In the Elizabethan period in England, a 'curber' or 'angler' was a thief who used a hook to take up items through open windows or from market stalls, and he or she might also be referred to as a hooker. True, an opportunist thief is not the same as a prostitute, but there is the element of surreptitious activity in both trades coupled with, in the case of the prostitute, the idea of the lure, hooking the client in. And the term 'hook' is still used in fields like advertising or filmmaking to describe the device or trick which will catch the attention of a potential customer.

TO HAVE A FIVE-TO-SEVEN (FRENCH)

Avoir/se faire un cinq à sept – to have an assignation with a lover

This idiom comes from the 19th century, when your average *bourgeois gentilhomme*, with plenty of time on his hands and a reputation for philandering to maintain, set aside commerce and went to visit his mistress in the late afternoon. Thence to return to the bosom of his family as evening fell.

How delightfully French! A quickie, but one lasting a full two hours – the sexual equivalent of a lazy Gallic lunch. It's anyone's guess whether the practice has survived into these more pressurised times, or if it died out with the *belle époque*. But it's tempting to imagine that, while his British, American or German counterpart is slaving over a hot spreadsheet, the Frenchman is still sloping off for an illicit frolic. Ever wondered, for instance, why the 35-hour week was pioneered in France?

In Francophone Canada, *cinq à sept* has a quite different meaning: a 'happy hour', generally on Thursdays, when bars offer drinks priced at two for one. Québécois working in Paris, take note: be careful what you invite your colleagues to.

TO HAVE AN EARWORM (GERMAN)

Einen Ohrwurm haben – **to be unable to get a tune out of your head**

The 2003 film *Touching the Void*, the true story of British climbers Joe Simpson and Simon Yates' calamitous ascent of Siula Grande in the Andes in 1985, contains an exquisite moment of black humour. Left for dead by his partner after breaking a leg and plunging 100 feet into a crevasse, Simpson drags himself the five miles back to base camp across a glacier. Near the end of this agonising journey, from nowhere the strains of *Brown Girl in the Ring*, an infuriating disco ditty from the 1970s, float into his delirious mind. It infuriates Simpson into making one last superhuman effort to reach safety before Yates breaks camp: the sole thought in his head is 'bloody hell…I'm not going to die listening to Boney M.'. Indeed, hard to imagine a worse fate.

Here, then, in its most extreme form, is the earworm. The graphic image of a parasitic tune burrowing its way into your skull is so powerful that, since the early 2000s, English has adopted the German term and made it its own. And the defining characteristic of an earworm is its sheer God-awfulness. You'll never hear anyone lamenting that they can't dislodge a Schubert impromptu or a Bach cello sonata from their head. No, earworms skulk at the very bottom of the musical pond – the more moronic forms of pop or, even worse, advertising jingles. The top three of 2006, as listed by James Kellaris, professor of marketing at the University of Cincinnati and the man largely responsible for popularising the concept, were as follows: Kylie Minogue's *Can't Get You Out of My Head* (appropriately enough); James Blunt's *You're Beautiful*; and the Baha Men's *Who Let the Dogs Out*. Enough said.

But was Simpson at least grateful for the motivating aversion therapy provided by *Brown Girl in the Ring*? Was he Hell. As he explains ruefully on his website:

> *My taste in music does not run to Boney M. It was a dreadful song and I think it was a last desperate ruse by my brain to keep me hanging in there. Ironically we had to pay them £25,000 to use that clip of awful music because it was re-mixed. Still can't believe I've managed to line their pockets.*

SWEET FANNY ADAMS/SWEET FA (UK)
Said to denote something which is of no value/nothing at all

The stories behind idioms are sometimes rather more grim than their superficial sense suggests (e.g. to break a butterfly on a wheel) but there can be few more unpleasant than the explanation which lies behind 'Sweet Fanny Adams'. On a summer's afternoon in 1867, the eight-year-old Fanny Adams was abducted in Alton, Hampshire. Her decapitated, mutilated and dismembered body was very soon found in a hopfield and by the late evening a solicitor's clerk had been taken into custody. All the evidence pointed towards Frederick Baker, from the bloodstains on his clothing to a chillingly flat diary entry ('Saturday 24, killed a young girl; it was fine and hot.'). Baker was tried, found guilty by a jury within 15 minutes and hanged outside Winchester Gaol before a crowd of 5,000 people on the morning of Christmas Eve, 1867. His was one of the last public executions in the United Kingdom. Shortly afterwards, the Royal Navy started to issue ships' crews with meat that was tinned instead of being preserved by salting. The mutton inside the tins was evidently not to the sailors' taste and, with grim humour, they were said to contain the remains of 'Sweet Fanny Adams'. The idea that human flesh could be passed off as meat seems to have been a minor but recurring feature of Victorian urban legend. The victims of the fictitious Sweeney Todd ended up as the filling for meat pies, while shortly after the grisly death of Fanny Adams, the name of another murder victim, the adult Harriet Lane, was used as a slang phrase for tinned meat.

Then the story of the unfortunate Fanny Adams (FA) became tangled up with the abbreviation for 'fuck all', or rather it must have been observed that they have the same initials. 'Fuck' as a taboo word has existed for centuries but 'fuck all' first appears towards the end of the Victorian era. By the end of the First World War and in the forms FA or Sweet FA this revised expression is noted as meaning 'nothing', 'no result'. To an extent, 'Sweet Fanny Adams/ Sweet FA' can be regarded as a euphemism rather like 'flipping heck' (standing for 'fucking hell') since it avoids the direct utterance of a taboo word. But the real story behind this idiom is actually more disturbing than any swear word could be.

THROW YOUR HAT OVER THE WINDMILLS
(FRENCH)

Jeter son bonnet par-dessus des moulins – **to give in (archaic)/ to let your hair down; fly in the face of convention**

A perplexing idiom, this, with a long and varied history. Its first attested use is in 1640 by Antoine Oudin, a linguist and intellectual at the court of Louis XIII, who identified it in his *Curiosités françaises* as a formulaic phrase used by people when they found themselves at a loss how to finish a story. When telling a child a made-up bedtime tale, for instance, you could wrap things up by saying *Et je jette mon bonnet…*: something akin to 'And no one knows what became of them.'/'But that's another story'.

Over time, the idiom took on an entirely different sense, so that by the 19th century, it came to denote someone deliberately cocking a snook at public opinion. More particularly, it was used of young women who had 'gone to the bad' and shamelessly transgressed the bounds of propriety. The connotation of sexual licence is clear in the image of hair tumbling free from underneath a bonnet thus hurled: the outmoded French term *une femme en cheveux* meant 'a woman of ill-repute'. Plus, in Orthodox Judaism, Islam, and certain conservative sects, it is strictly taboo for adult females to show their uncovered hair to anyone but their husbands. A powerful metaphor, then, for a woman gaily abandoning her virginity.

But the 'windmills' of the idiom, in either its archaic or its more recent sense, remain unexplained. They appear to be there solely for heightening effect, not unlike (in the latter case) the English phrase 'throwing caution to the wind'.

There are, interestingly, two references in the works of Oscar Wilde to women 'throwing their caps/bonnets over the mills'. Lady Narborough in the novel *The Picture of Dorian Grey* (1891) and Mr. Dumby in the play *Lady Windermere's Fan* (1892) both use it to describe people who have flown in the face of convention in pursuit of love. It would appear that, at least for a spell, Victorian England adopted the loan usage from French as a euphemism for women losing their virtue.

FROM BEHIND, A GIRLS' SCHOOL, FROM THE FRONT A MUSEUM (GERMAN)

Von hinten Lyzeum, von vorne Museum – 'mutton dressed as lamb'

This is a sexist little item, expressing male disappointment on discovering that a woman who appeared to be worth lusting after is in fact much older than she first seemed. There's plenty to outrage here: first, the body-fascist premise that only slimness is attractive (something men don't pay much attention to in their own health regime, it must be said); second, the pervy exaltation of schoolgirls as the ideal of feminine beauty; and finally the blithe assumption that no mature woman could possibly be worth a second look. And overarching all this – in both the German phrase and its English translation – a tone of lofty disdain suggesting that any attempts by women 'of a certain age' to care for their appearance are risible and doomed to failure.

But in purely linguistic terms, it's snappy and inventive, and so warrants inclusion here. A marginally less offensive variant runs: *Von hinten Blondine, von vorne Ruine*: 'from behind, a hot blonde. From the front, a ruin.'

PUT YOUR HAND IN THE FIRE FOR SOMEONE/SOMETHING (ITALIAN)

Mettere la mano sul fuoco per qualcuno/qualcosa – to vouch for someone/to swear to or guarantee something

The ancient city of Rome's struggle to break a siege by the semi-legendary Etruscan tyrant Lars Porsena of Clusium (modern Chiusi) in c.508–507 BC provided more than its fair share of heroic archetypes. One such was Horatius who, having destroyed the bridge over the Tiber in order to prevent

Porsena's forces from entering Rome, found himself stranded on the far side of the river and had to swim back in full armour to his jubilant compatriots. The historian and poet Lord Macaulay made the episode famous in his 1842 *Lays of Ancient Rome* ('…and even the ranks of Tuscany could scarce forbear to cheer').

Another doughty Roman from this conflict was the youth Gaius Mucius Cordus, who was sanctioned by the Senate to infiltrate the Etruscan camp and murder Lars Porsena. And he almost pulled it off, reaching the leader's tent but stabbing his secretary by mistake. Seized and threatened with torture and death, Mucius pre-empted his fate by thrusting the hand that he blamed for misdirecting him to the wrong target into a campfire, scorching it to a crisp. Porsena was so impressed by this display of fearlessness and unquestioning loyalty to Rome that he released his young foe; back in Rome, Mucius was rewarded for his feat with the cognomen *Scaevola* ('left-handed') and granted a tract of land across the Tiber, the *Mucia Prata* ('Mucian meadows'). In addition, Mucius' assertion when captured that there were 300 more assassins like him waiting in the wings so unnerved Porsena that he lifted the siege and sued for peace.

The idiom continues to be used (in German as well: *Für ihn würde ich meine Hand ins Feuer legen*) to express unswerving trust in a person or fact. On its journey to the present day, it may have been reinforced by the medieval judicial practice of 'trial by fire', in which the accused was obliged to grasp a red-hot iron bar. The absence of any resulting injury was taken as proof of innocence (*See* **Catch-22**).

PRESS MY THUMBS! (German)

Drück mir die Daumen! – fingers crossed/wish me luck!

Originating in the super-superstitious Middle Ages, or possibly in even older Germanic folklore, the invitation to press a person's thumbs is thought to be related to the idea of the thumb as a 'lucky finger', and that touching thumbs with another would help banish demons and nightmares. An alternative explanation in this same realm has thumbs, rather, as a repository of demonic powers, which could only be held in check by pressing.

On a totally different tack, the phrase may relate to the practice of *pollice verso* – the Roman emperors' famous hand gesture signalling clemency or condemnation of gladiators in the Colosseum. This is certainly the derivation of the ubiquitous 'thumb's up' sign of approval.

Sadly, then, this is another idiom in the 'anyone's guess' category... But it's worth noting that there may be a very sound physiological basis for such superstitious reverence of this particular digit; after all, it's our possession of opposable thumbs that gives us humans our unique manual dexterity in the animal kingdom, and has assured us (along with our brain size and bipedal posture) our rip-roaring evolutionary success.

The Italians have a nice equivalent: *In Bocca al lupo!* ('Into the wolf's mouth!'). To which the appropriate response is: *Crepi il lupo!* ('May the wolf die!' – with the implied meaning 'hope he chokes on me!').

A FLEA IN YOUR EAR

As a universal parasite that made people's lives an itching, scratching misery in the days before improvements in public hygiene and advances in insecticides, fleas were bound to enter into popular phraseology. Far worse than the constant irritation they brought, rat fleas were the vector of the bacterium *Yersinia pestis*, which caused the Black Death. But putting a flea in someone's ear has a subtly different meaning in France, Germany and the United Kingdom.

The idea of sending someone away with a flea in their ear, as it is usually expressed in English, indicates a sharp rebuke. *Mettre la puce à l'oreille*, on the other hand, means 'to set someone thinking', with the particular nuance of planting the seeds of suspicion or alarm in their head[1].

Commensurate with this, *avoir la puce à l'oreille* suggests that you've got a nasty feeling about something, or more generally that you're all het up. For many centuries (but no longer), this idiom had the very particular sense of being sexually restless, somewhat akin to our 'seven-year itch'.

The German *jemandem einen Floh ins Ohr setzen* is broadly similar to the French but, rather than harbouring a sense of foreboding, it means that you've instilled an *idée fixe* in the person concerned. This notion is also conveyed by the phrase *einen Floh im Ohr haben* – 'to have a bee in your bonnet', i.e. to be not in your right mind.

---

1 The Italian *mettere la pulce nel'orecchio* also has this same force.

Whatever the nuance, the idea of this nasty little bloodsucker in your lughole is deeply unpleasant. But as the Germans say (particularly the inhabitants of the former GDR), *Lieber einen Floh im Ohr als eine Wanze im Telefon*: 'better a flea in your ear than a bug in your 'phone.'

Chapter 12

THE LONG ARM OF THE LAW

Slang and idioms which derive from criminal or quasi-legal activity have always been popular – with people on the right side of the law, that is. Films, TV, books and comics popularise criminal-related expressions today just as Elizabethan guides and dictionaries did 400 years ago. Crime buffs absorb expressions from their favourite writers and shows. For instance, they know from Raymond Chandler's detective novels that 'gat' is US slang for 'gun' and also that its heyday was during the 1940s, since when it has been replaced by expressions such as 'piece' or 'heat'. Drug-dealing and drug-taking have pawned hundreds of expressions, a few of which like 'pot', 'crack' or 'shoot up' have entered mainstream English and so enlarged the language. Of all forms of slang, thieves' jargon or cant, as it was once known, is surely the most dramatic because it seems to provide a glimpse of a closed and dangerous world. In this section are to be found a few terms drawn from the United States; always a fertile source for the language of crime.

TAKE THE PERP WALK (US)

To be paraded in public by the police, usually after an arrest but before a trial

Fans of US crime drama are likely to be well versed in abbreviations and argot such as DUI (driving under the influence), DOA (dead on arrival), vic(tim) and perp(etrator). The perp is sometimes subjected to the 'perp walk' and,

American justice being more open than its British cousin, this is the system at its most brutally transparent. In a country where the order to cross or not to cross the road is a peremptory 'Walk/Don't Walk' and where jaywalking is a crime, the perp walk is an additional humiliation for the offender as he – and it's usually a 'he' – is escorted a short distance on foot, in cuffs and in public, for the benefit of the cameras. The ostensible reason for the perp walk is to transfer the alleged offender from A to B, from police car to police station or courthouse. But the underlying reason is to expose the frequently unshaven, dishevelled malefactor to the public gaze, and the humiliation which results from that exposure is part of the punishment, even though most perp-walkers are not yet convicted.

High-grade white-collar wrongdoers commonly receive the treatment, as a way of rubbing their noses in their fall from grace and as a demonstration of the equality of all before the law. Men like the Enron fraudsters, Ken Lay and Jeffrey Skilling, and the ex-chairman of the IMF, Dominique Strauss-Kahn, have all been perp-walked. If you don't know what it means, doing the perp walk might sound a vaguely jolly activity, something in the style of a 1960s dance like the Watusi (or the Twist), but it can have disastrous consequences, as it did on 24 November 1963. In the basement of the Dallas police headquarters, the authorities – eager to show they had found the assassin of President John F. Kennedy – led Lee Harvey Oswald past a television crew broadcasting live. Oswald was shot and killed by nightclub owner Jack Ruby and history was denied the chance to discover Oswald's motives and (perhaps) to avoid decades of conspiracy theories and theorists. The 'perp walk' expression has been picked up in the United Kingdom only recently and, in newspaper references, may be accompanied by an explanation as well as being enclosed in quotation marks. But as it becomes more familiar, the explanations and the sanitising inverted commas will drop away.

THIRD DEGREE (US)
Harsh questioning, probably involving mistreatment

As a phrase, the 'third degree' was coined more than 150 years ago to describe the harsh interrogation of a suspect by the police. A reference in *The New York Times* in 1910 has a senior policeman denying that 'the so-called "sweating" or "third degree" system' is practised in the United States. The implication is that the third degree is not far from torture. But an earlier turn-of-the-century article in the same newspaper describes the system at length, and suggests that the third degree is less to do with brutality than with the seniority of the policemen involved. According to this account, the first degree is to be questioned by precinct officers, while the second brings in a detective from headquarters and the third means a 'big examination' by the chief of the detective bureau and his subordinates. Of the examples given, only one concerns physical mistreatment, when a suspected bond thief was put into a cell during August and a stove was lit to keep the temperature uncomfortably high. After three weeks, during which the prisoner lost 22 pounds as a result of perspiration (the original 'sweating' perhaps), the thief confessed. The other cases of the third degree are more to with trickery, either by recreating a crime scene or by 'pampering' the suspect so that he is taken off-guard and gives himself away.

Whatever the subtleties of the application of the third degree in early 20th century US policing, the phrase has generally signified rough treatment. One explanation for its source is that it is a reference to the stages through which a freemason has to pass before reaching the third level of master mason, the most demanding degree of all. Another etymology has the phrase coined by a veteran New York detective chief called Thomas Byrnes who was punning on his name and third-degree burns.

TAKE THE FIFTH (US)
To avoid giving evidence which might incriminate oneself

The fifth amendment to the United States constitution, one of a list of 10 amendments known collectively as the Bill of Rights, gives protection to the citizen from abuses in the application of the law. For example, it states that an individual can't be tried twice for the same offence (the 'double jeopardy' rule). But the specific clause in the amendment invoked by those who take or 'plead the fifth' is the right to stay silent under oath if the answers could incriminate the person being questioned: 'nor shall [any person] be compelled in any criminal case to be a witness against himself.' This does not extend to the incrimination of others nor does it apply to other kinds of oral, self-incriminating evidence which have been compelled, such as voice samples or breath tests for alcohol. 'Taking the fifth' is a legitimate option when appearing in court or before congressional committees etc., and juries are warned that nothing (i.e. guilt) should be inferred from the silence of the witness. A similar protective system operates when suspects are arrested by the police and read their rights, including the right to say nothing. These are known as Miranda rights, from a Supreme Court case in the 1960s involving Ernesto Miranda, and the transitive verb form, to mirandise, is quite often seen and heard.

THREE STRIKES (AND YOU'RE OUT) (US)
Originally a baseball term and now signifying that after three criminal offences, the punishment will be extreme, perhaps up to life imprisonment

One of several expressions from baseball which have entered mainstream American English, the phrase 'three strikes and you're out' describes the penalty paid by the batter after three failed attempts to hit the ball. Its metaphorical application arises from an attempt to deal with repeat criminals when many US states enacted laws in the 1990s requiring mandatory and extended prison sentences for those committing a third serious offence. In some states, however, the third conviction could result from a relatively minor infringement. Not surprisingly, the blanket imposition of the law led to harsh penalties for a few. In California, a state which was particularly fervent in applying the 'three strikes' rule, a man with two previous robbery convictions was sentenced to 25 years to life for attempting to prise open the doors of a soup kitchen because he was homeless and hungry (he was released after 13 years). The phrase is not much found outside the United States, although it is sometimes used to describe attempts by UK legislators or other authorities to crack down on offences such as benefit fraud or Internet piracy.

THREE TIMES IS MARITIME LAW (DUTCH)
Driemaal is scheepsrecht – **third time lucky**

No one knows why the number three should, since time immemorial, have had such strong connotations of good fortune. There may be some vague connection with the Holy Trinity, but there's nothing to corroborate this idea. Where the English phrase is concerned, the compiler of the

Phrasefinder website (phrases.org.uk) discusses, but soon dismisses, the folk wisdom that the idiom can be traced back to a law supposedly granting pardon to any condemned man who survived three attempts at hanging him (no such statute ever existed).

The Dutch idiom takes us to a realm rich in superstition: the sea and seafaring. Maritime practice in the Netherlands from the Middle Ages onwards yields several well-attested examples of rewards, or punishments, on board ship being meted out in groups of three. A captain, for instance, was obliged to provide his crew with three meals a day. Disorderly behaviour in the mess room was customarily punished with three blows from a *gortspann*, a short hooked wooden club for pummelling cooked grain. And finally, the bodies of sailors who died during passage were committed to the deep with the words *Een, twee, drie, in Gods naam* ('One, two, three, in the name of God'). All interesting stuff, for sure, but the fundamental mystery as to why three was so indelibly associated with luck remains unsolved.

SMOKING GUN (US)
Providing undeniable proof of complicity or guilt

The smoking gun is obviously one which has just been fired and, if still in the grasp of the shooter, then it provides crystal-clear evidence against him or her. It is the equivalent of being caught red-handed. The American newspaper columnist William Safire traced the first appearance of a smoking gun as evidence to a Sherlock Holmes tale, *The Gloria Scott* (1893). In this short story, convicts on a ship bound for Australia overpower the crew and a fake chaplain commits murder: 'Then we rushed on into the captain's cabin, but as we pushed

THE LONG ARM OF THE LAW 213

open the door there was an explosion from within, and there
he lay with his head on the chart of the Atlantic [...] while the
chaplain stood with a smoking pistol in his hand... .'

The association with crime is apparent enough – a hardboiled detective thriller entitled *The Mystery of the Smoking
Gun* appeared in 1936 – but the metaphorical popularity of
the expression really boomed at the time of the Watergate
scandal which finished the presidency of Richard Nixon in
1974. The tape recording which revealed Nixon in a
conspiracy with members of his entourage to cajole the FBI
into abandoning its investigation of the Watergate break-in
became known as the 'smoking gun' tape. This was because it
contained evidence of the obstruction of justice, an offence
which was sufficient grounds for Nixon's impeachment (in
the event, Nixon resigned before he could be impeached).
Ever since, the phrase has continued to be popular both in a
legal context – a prosecutor might be lucky enough to find
himself with a 'once-a-year smoking-gun' case, as the *New
York Times* put it – as well as more widely applicable in
international relations. In the 1980s, there were attempts to
find the 'smoking gun' which would show the involvement
of the Soviet Union in chemical warfare. The fruitless search
before and after the 2003 invasion of Iraq to prove that
Saddam Hussein was making and hiding weapons of mass
destruction became the archetypal quest for a 'smoking gun'.
The phrase reached its apogee in the statement by
Condoleezza Rice: 'We don't want the smoking gun to be a
mushroom cloud.'

The 'smoking gun' can be given a light-hearted twist,
however, reinforced by the obvious connection to the
proverbial 'where's there's smoke, there's fire'. Any

compromising communication now is more likely to be found online than on tape and, if so, is termed a 'smoking e-mail'. Nor is it a surprise that, given his reputation, Bill Clinton's staff were said to be constantly on the lookout for 'smoking bimbos' while, if a scandal broke, the result could be a 'bimbo eruption'.

KANGAROO COURT (US)

An unofficial court providing a 'trial' which is far from fair

Although the kangaroo is an exclusively Australian animal, the strange hybrid which is the 'kangaroo court' hops into view in Texas in a book published in 1853: 'By a unanimous vote, Judge G—— was elected to the bench and the "Mestang" or "Kangaroo Court" regularly organized' (Philip Paxton, *A Stray Yankee in Texas*). The humorous story behind this describes a mock trial played out among lawyers during a 'court week' in a frontier county town. The object of their after-hours session is to get someone to pay for the drinks at the bar and in the end it is Judge G who is found 'guilty' and must pay up. To the extent that the kangaroo court is conducted by members of the bar, in another sense, this is a semi-official proceeding, albeit a humorous one. But 'kangaroo' references later in the 19th century show that any such court is more likely to be found inside a gaol, as a system for forcing money out of new prisoners. Current usage of the phrase extends to any body which acts like a tribunal and whose proceedings are regarded as irregular or blatantly unjust.

But why the kangaroo? Most explanations owe more to ingenuity than good sense. The fixed stare of the kangaroo might be compared with the gaze of a judge; or the shifting of a court from place to place is like the hopping of a kangaroo, and so on. A more plausible connection is to the unpredictable, even uncontrollable nature of the beast – an idea reinforced by the parallel reference to 'mestang' in the quotation above, since the mustang is the wild horse of the American prairies. Perhaps there's a sidelong glance, too, at the kangaroo's oddity. The creature already figured in US metaphors as early as 1848, around the time when many Australians arrived in California during the gold rush. A 'kangaroo ticket' described the duo campaigning for the highest political offices if the man standing for vice president was seen as a more appealing prospect than the one aspiring to be president. The virtue of such a campaign was said to reside, like the kangaroo's strength, in its hind legs. This endearingly bizarre image was still in use in the 1990s.

THE MAFIA

The range of expressions from the whole apparatus of American crime, whether from the side of the criminals or the upholders of the law, is rich and varied. The worldwide success of the book and film of *The Godfather*, and the long-running television series *The Sopranos*, made the mafia into an organisation simultaneously frightening and exotic, and put a slew of phrases into general circulation. They range from *omertà* (the vow of silence) to *consigliere* (the adviser) to the wiseguys and the made men, those who have been initiated into the organisation, to such quotes as 'Sleep with the fishes' or Marlon Brando's 'I'll make him an offer he can't refuse' or 'Just when I thought I was out...they pull me back in' (a line from Al Pacino in

Godfather III which is echoed/parodied by Steven van Zandt's character in *The Sopranos*). The distant origins of the term 'Mafia' are disputed, although its immediate source is as a piece of Sicilian dialect. It may date back as far as the Arabic occupation of the island in the 9th century and be a version of an Arabic word for either 'bragging' or 'outcast'.

Chapter 13

TRAVELLERS' TALES

Idiomatic language is by its very nature colourful and pictorial. Its stock-in-trade includes famous or eccentric people, notable events and playfully surreal images. Small wonder, then, that it should also deal in memorable places, encapsulating what has latterly been called 'psychogeography' – the essential qualities that define a particular location.

Idioms can fix forever aspects of a city or region that have long since disappeared or drifted from their original anchorage. Instances of this from the United Kingdom and Ireland are 'coals to Newcastle', a 'London particular', 'Brummagem ware' and '[to fight like] Kilkenny cats'. We have chosen to focus here, though, on some of the more memorable examples from abroad, ranging from puns on the names of Belgian towns and a Central American state, through Italian regional rivalries (still a live issue) to the financial history of Ancient Greece.

The only appropriate place to end this overview was somewhere that has no real existence at all, the fool's paradise of a Land of Plenty, which has gone by various names down the ages.

GO TO CANOSSA (Italian)

Andare a Canossa – **to eat humble pie**

The Investiture Controversy – the conflict between Europe's temporal and spiritual rulers over who had the authority to appoint bishops – came to a head in 1076. At a synod convened in the German city of Worms that year, Pope Gregory VII, frustrated at what he saw as the attempted secular domination of the Church by the German King Henry IV, declared him deposed and excommunicated him. The Pope's edict absolved 'all Christians from the bond of the oath they had made' to Henry.

In the early Middle Ages, a papal denunciation carried real clout and Henry found his authority ebbing away. Realising he'd have to sue for peace with Gregory or lose his throne, in January 1077 he journeyed to the northern Italian stronghold of Canossa, where the Pope was staying as a guest of Matilda of Tuscany, to offer his unconditional submission. Gregory saw no reason to go easy on the penitent Henry and kept him waiting outside the castle, barefoot and hair-shirted in the snow of a bitter winter, for three whole days and nights before granting him an audience and absolving him of his sins.

Revenge is a dish best served cold. In 1084, having resumed hostilities against the Papacy, Henry marched on Rome, took the city, installed his own biddable antipope Clement III (who invested him as Holy Roman Emperor), and banished Gregory, who died in exile in Salerno the following year.

But it was the king's public humiliation that stuck in the medieval mind and became a byword for profound self-abasement. Significantly, the idiom also lives on in German, in the phrase *ein Gang nach Canossa* ('a walk to Canossa').

CARRY OWLS TO ATHENS (German)

Eulen nach Athen tragen – **to take coals to Newcastle**

In his comedy *Birds*, the 4th-century BC Greek dramatist Aristophanes has his character Euelpides ask incredulously

'Who brings owls to Athens?' (*glauk'eis Athenas*). The implication is that the city has plenty already. Owls, which once roosted in the rafters of the old Parthenon (the one burned by Xerxes I of Persia during his invasion of Greece a few decades before the playwright's birth in 480 BC), were so strongly associated with Athens that they became the symbol of its patron deity Athena, goddess of wisdom. And as the quintessential Athenian mascot, the owl appeared on the reverse of the silver drachmae minted by the city. These were commonly referred to as *glaukai*.

Not only was it a foolish enterprise, then, to literally take owls to Athens, but also figuratively to try to bring coins back to what was the centre of the Hellenistic world and the source of all its wealth. In this sense, owl-carrying isn't the absurd activity it first appears, but clearly has the same force as the English idiom 'taking coals to Newcastle', i.e. a counter-productive economic activity. Aristophanes wasn't criticising some harmless idiosyncrasy but instead was making a trenchant satirical point. Over centuries, Greek mercantile activity had established the Attic tetradrachm as the hard currency of choice throughout the eastern Mediterranean – the Yankee dollar of the ancient Levant. But its high silver content had also made it popular with speculators and hoarders, who began to flood the home market with the coinage. To Aristophanes, the owl had become the symbol of boundless excess and greed.

As well as 'coals to Newcastle', first used in the 16th century, modern variants include the Spanish *dar trigo a Castilla* ('to give wheat [= metaphorically, money] to Castille') and the French *emporter les femmes à Paris*.

CROSS THE RUBICON (UK)

To take an irrevocable step

This expression has existed in English for hundreds of years although it was more often seen in the form of 'pass the Rubicon'. It refers to a crucial moment in Roman history in 49 BC when Julius Caesar was engaged in a power struggle with Pompey the Great. Pompey influenced the Senate to declare Caesar an enemy of the state. In response, Caesar led his army across the Rubicon, a river that formed a boundary between the province of Cisalpine Gaul, of which he was governor, and the north-east of Italy. Once he crossed the frontier, Caesar was violating a law, intended to prevent a *coup d'état*, which barred any general from bringing his forces into Italy proper. It was beginning of a civil war which Caesar won and which, in the longer term, marked the end of the Roman republic and the start of centuries of rule by a succession of emperors. Shortly before ordering his forces across the river, Julius Caesar is reputed to have said 'alea iacta est' or 'the die [dice] is cast'.

As a river boundary, the Rubicon never lived up to its significance in history since, even in Caesar's time, it was a minor waterway. The name, however, has a continued resonance and sometimes appears by itself to signal a point of no return. *Rubicon* was used as the title of an intriguing US television series in 2010, about a conspiracy of arms manufacturers manipulating world events for their profit. The title was a subtle contemporary nod at Caesar's historical action in bringing the military into civilian affairs, perhaps too subtle since *Rubicon* was cancelled after only one season. As an idiom, 'crossing the Rubicon' is related to 'burn one's boats' or 'burn one's bridges', both of them having war-like overtones and indicating an irrevocable course from which retreat is impossible. A key feature of these expressions is that there is a voluntary element to them: Caesar chose to cross the Rubicon. (see also **Draw a line in the sand**)

MENIN IS CLOSE TO COURTRAI (BUT FAR FROM WAREGEM) (Dutch/Flemish)

Menen ligt dicht bij Kortrijk (maar verre van Waregem) –
'thinking' something isn't the same as 'knowing' it

Menin in West Flanders is now indelibly associated in English with the carnage of the First World War. One of the most evocative paintings of the conflict, a blasted landscape of water-filled shell holes and decapitated trees painted by Paul Nash in 1919, is entitled *The Menin Road*. More famously, the principal memorial in the town of Ieper (also in the same province), featuring the names of almost 55,000 Commonwealth soldiers who died without graves at the Ypres Salient, is the Menin Gate.

This phrase relates to Menin's even closer proximity to yet another West Flanders town: Kortrijk, or Courtrai, and turns on a double pun. *Menen* is not only the Dutch/Flemish name for Menin but also the infinitive of the verb meaning 'to think, to reckon'. Similarly, Waregem is a town that lies further afield, on the border between West and East Flanders; its name hints at the Dutch adjective *waar* ('true'). So, if someone responded to a question where certainty was required by saying 'I think that…', they could immediately be stopped in their tracks with this snappy (if rather bumptious) put-down.

BE LEFT UNDER THE MOON OF VALENCIA
(SPANISH)

Quedarse a la luna de Valencia – **to be disappointed/left in the lurch/left high and dry**

This idiom has two derivations, both historical. The first relates to the impressive medieval fortifications of this ancient Spanish city. In former times, when a curfew was observed, all the gates in the city walls would be shut at 10 in the evening and remain firmly closed until the following morning. Anyone seeking access at night, for however innocent a reason, would be refused entry and forced to kick their heels outside for the whole night, with only the cold moonlight for company. Plausible enough, but surely there were plenty of walled cities where such a scene could have been played out? Why Valencia in particular?

The second derivation brings us, once again, to that abiding obsession of Spanish phraseology – the Moors. Or more precisely in this case, the *moriscos* (literally 'Moor-like'), those forcibly converted Muslims who had stayed in Spain after most of their coreligionists had been expelled after the Catholic reconquest (*Reconquista*) of the country was completed with the fall of Granada in 1492. Over the following centuries, the *moriscos* and their Christianised Jewish counterparts the *marranos* (a pejorative term meaning 'swine') acted as convenient scapegoats whenever crisis loomed, whether real or imaginary. So it was in 1609 when a threatening Ottoman presence in the Mediterranean raised fears of the 'enemy within' making common cause with a Turkish–French Huguenot alliance against Spain. This prompted King Philip III and the Viceroy of Valencia, Archbishop Juan de Ribera, to order the immediate expulsion of the 135,000 *moriscos* in the city and the surrounding region.

A main embarkation point for the refugees, who were stripped of all their wealth and permitted to take only what they could carry, was the shoreline just outside Valencia. The vessels that arrived to take them to destinations such as Oran in Algeria and Tunis were soon filled to the gunwales and set sail, leaving thousands behind. And although promises were made that the ships would return, few were kept. Many *moriscos* began the long trek to France, settling in Marseilles. Thereafter, the powerful image of the destitute horde left to languish under the moon of Valencia came to epitomise a state of being left in the lurch.

IN THE STICKS (US)

Describing the world outside urban centres; provincial

This slightly disparaging expression for any distant rural area beyond the metropolitan centres originated in the United States but is quite common in British English, although media use tends to be ironic or knowing, as in the film festival event titled 'Flicks in the Sticks'. The 'sticks' reference is to trees, and the association between uncultivated land, the darkness of woods and the supposedly simple lives of their inhabitants is an old one. A similar idea is implicit in 'backwoodsman' (backwoods originally meaning uncleared forest), which in the US may define a rugged, frontier-style countryman but which can also carry associations of simplicity and ignorance. In the United Kingdom, the word has a specialised application to a member of the House of Lords who rarely attends sessions.

A parallel expression to 'in the sticks' is 'in the boonies' or 'boondocks'. This derives from *bundock*, a Tagalog word meaning hill or mountain, and one picked up by American fighters in the Philippines during the Spanish-American War

(1898). The boondocks are not necessarily mountainous but they are always remote from cities and underpopulated.

BE BETWEEN PINTO AND VALDEMORO
(Spanish)

Estar entre Pinto y Valdemoro – **to be in two minds/ to be sozzled**

Odd that an idiom should have two such different meanings: what's the connection?

Let's tackle the second sense first, as arguably the less interesting line of enquiry. This goes back to an old folk tale. Pinto and Valdemoro are towns some 15 kilometres due south of the centre of Madrid, and only about three kilometres distant from one another. The story concerns a notorious former inhabitant of the then-village of Pinto who was both a drunkard and a simpleton. His party piece was to accompany people to a stream on the outskirts of the village marking the boundary between the communes of Pinto and Valdemoro, and leap back and forth across it, shouting 'Now I'm in Pinto!...Now I'm in Valdemoro!'. One time, missing his footing and landing squarely in the brook, he announced, unfazed: 'Now I'm between Pinto and Valdemoro!' The idiom as a euphemism for drunkenness commemorates this legendary boozer and his droll antics.

But the basic idea of the borderline at the heart of this anecdote is responsible for the phrase's more general usage to signal a state of being 'neither here nor there'. Here, we encounter two interesting and plausible explanations of its origin. The first concerns the period when Spain was ruled by the Habsburg dynasty (1506–1700). The road south from the capital through Pinto and Valdemoro carries on to Aranjuez, site of a grand royal palace commissioned by the most illustrious Spanish Habsburg, Philip II, and built by the same architect who designed the Escorial (see **To prepare yourself for St-Quentin**). Because Aranjuez lay almost 50 km from the centre of Madrid – more than a day's ride away, in other words – royal retinues would often stay over in Valdemoro. Allegedly, though, there was a house of ill-repute on the road just north of the village which was favoured by one of the Habsburg monarchs as his overnight billet. Whenever courtiers were quizzed over the whereabouts of the king (see also *Be in Babia*), they were wont to give the noncommittal reply 'between Pinto and Valdemoro'. In other words, a deliberate piece of prevarication and 'sitting on the fence'.

The second etymology relating to two minds has to do with drink, but not drunkenness. Particularly in the 19th century, wines from Valdemoro gained a reputation for excellence, so much so that they were regularly in demand at the Royal Court. As the French will tell you, *terroir* is everything in viticulture and wine from Pinto, despite its proximity to Valdemoro, was an altogether rougher item. And so, if a person really didn't want to proffer a definite opinion, in reference to these two extremes of wine-drinking pleasure, they'd describe something as being '*entre Pinto y Valdemoro*'.

GO TO NAPLES! (ITALIAN)
Va/vai a Napoli! – **go to hell!/fuck off!**

Italian politics is not only notoriously unstable (a comic once quipped 'Got a brilliant job during my gap year: Prime Minister of Italy') but is also fraught with regional antagonisms. While it's now considered bad form to stiletto or poison your opponents, with his 'Northern League' – founded in 1991

– Umberto Bossi created a party whose entire *raison d'être* is contemptuous hatred of the *mezzogiorno*, the south of the country. As early as 1806, the French traveller and Napoleonic administrator Augustin Creuzé de Lesser set the tone when he wrote in his *Voyage en Italie et Sicile* that 'Europe ends at Naples and ends there quite badly. Calabria, Sicily and all the rest belongs to Africa'.

Surprisingly, though, the dismissive phrase *Va a Napoli*, which implicitly equates Naples with Hell, wasn't coined by the callous sophisticates of Milan or Turin. Instead, it's born of an intraregional antipathy and comes from Sicily: going Up North, it appears, once rendered a Sicilian as good as dead. Neapolitans in particular were seen as stupid, vulgar peasants. Prior to unification, the island deeply resented being ruled from Naples in the state known as the Kingdom of the Two Sicilies (1811–61).

The phrase was inventively conflated by Sicilian immigrants to America with the commonplace Italian insult *vaffanculo* ('go fuck yourself') to create the new imprecation *vaffanapoli* (literally 'go and do Naples'). An elegant piece of linguistic artistry: while serving as a euphemism for the much coarser original, it also managed to be grossly more offensive to Neapolitans. It has even been abbreviated to *Fa nap*!

Poor Naples! The well-known phrase 'see Naples and die' (*Vedi Napoli e poi muori*), whose origins are obscure but are thought to lie in the city's Bourbon heyday (i.e. during the Kingdom of the Two Sicilies), was meant to convey the sense of 'Once you've seen Naples, you'll have seen the lot and can happily die'. But it's an obvious hostage to fortune: in his travel report *The Innocents Abroad* (1869) Mark Twain was already sneering, ' "SEE Naples and die?"

Well, I do not know that one would necessarily die after merely seeing it, but to attempt to live there might turn out a little differently.'

LEAVE GUATEMALA AND ARRIVE IN GUATEPEOR (SPANISH)

Salir de Guatemala y/para entrar en Guatepeor – **out of the frying pan into the fire**

A neat pun forms the heart of this Latin American Spanish phrase for going from a bad situation to one that is worse. The name of the Central American state of Guatemala, which is thought to derive from either the Maya-Toltec or the Nahuatl languages, contains by chance the Spanish adjective 'mala', meaning bad. Its comparative form 'peor' was then simply bolted onto the root to form the fictional place of Guatepeor ('Guate-worse').

Interestingly, Peninsular Spanish speakers tend to use the very similar phrase (but with place names nearer to home) *salir de Málaga para entrar/y meterse en Malagón*. In this instance, they are both real locations, with the augmentative suffix '–gon' heightening the force of *Mala*.

BUNK (US)

Nonsense/claptrap

'Bunk' is a shortened version of Buncombe, a county in North Carolina. For an explanation of how a place came to be synonymous with claptrap, it's necessary to go back to an 1820 debate in the US Congress on the Missouri Compromise, a contentious measure to do with slavery and the recognition of Missouri as a state. When North Carolina Representative Felix Walker stood up to address the House, his colleagues, knowing his reputation for bombastic speech, pleaded with him to be brief. Walker replied: 'I shall not be speaking to the House, but to Buncombe.' Soon 'buncombe' became a synonym for general waffle, though it also carried the sense of talking merely for the sake of making a good impression with one's constituents. By the end of the 19th century, the phonetic spelling of 'bunkum' lost its tail to turn into 'bunk', and the expression was famously employed by Henry Ford in an interview in the *Chicago Tribune*: 'History is more or less bunk.' (The qualifying 'more or less' is usually forgotten.)

The noun 'bunk' was the title of a satirical novel written in 1923 by William E. Woodward, who coined the opposing verb to 'debunk', meaning to chip away the humbug or false impressions surrounding a person or idea. This useful word also contributed to 'hokum', originally a piece of American theatrical slang and describing anything sentimental or pretentious. Hokum is probably a mashup of 'hocus-pocus' and 'bunkum', and is frequently coupled with the capital of filmmaking in the alliterative phrase 'Hollywood hokum'. The claptrap definition of 'bunk' is not related to the 'getaway' sense of the word – as in to 'do a bunk' – which probably comes from a Lincolnshire dialect term. Nor is it connected to the US 'bunco', deriving from a Spanish card game and meaning to cheat (a 'bunco artist' is a con man).

A PICTURE FROM ÉPINAL (French)
Une image d'Épinal – **an idealised, stereotypical depiction**

'The name Épinal on a signpost brings back another childish memory, of primitive coloured pictures and sheets of brightly uniformed soldiers, the *images d'Épinal* which have the same primitive charm as our penny-plain, twopence-coloured prints.'

Elizabeth David, *French Provincial Cooking* (1960)

The town of Épinal is situated in the Vosges *département* of the Lorraine region in eastern France. It lies on the River Moselle/Mosel, has around 35,000 inhabitants, and is twinned with Loughborough.

The sole claim to fame of this provincial backwater are the manufactures of the *Imagerie d'Épinal* printmaking works. Formerly the *Imagerie Pellerin*, roughly 200 years ago it began mass-producing stencil-coloured woodcuts and lithographs – a new departure, after its founder Jean-Charles Pellerin found that his original line in painting clock dials with religious motifs didn't pay. The engravings, printed on hand-operated letterpresses, presented stirring historical scenes from the French Revolution and the Napoleonic era, fairytale and comic characters (like Puss in Boots or Pierrette) and other folksy themes.

The *images d'Épinal* evoked an unchangingly idyllic view of France, where (to quote Dr Pangloss from Voltaire's *Candide*) all was for the best in the best of all possible worlds. Sentimentality sells, and they proved hugely popular. The press is still in business after a relaunch in 1984 but its heyday was between 1870 and 1914, when it turned out more than 10 million prints a year. It offers strong circumstantial evidence of a nation in denial, seeking solace in past glories after the humiliation of the Franco-Prussian War.

At some stage, the concept entered the idiomatic realm, describing a stereotypical portrayal that harps on only the positive aspects. It crops up often in the contemporary French media, usually by way of bursting the bubble of some politician or *apparatchik* peddling an impossibly rose-tinted version of events.

BE WORTH A POTOSÍ (SPANISH)

Valer un Potosí – **to be worth a fortune/mint**

When the Spanish *conquistadores* first arrived in the New World, their express intent was to enrich themselves with the limitless gold reputed to exist there. In Mexico, Hernán Cortés and his men took a large haul of golden artefacts – weighing 162,000 *pesos de oro*, or almost 20,000 troy ounces – when they sacked the Aztec capital of Tenochtitlán in 1521. Even better was to follow for Francisco Pizarro when he invaded Peru 11 years later; the Inca ruler Atahuallpa tried (in vain) to buy his freedom with a roomful of gold, supposedly totalling seven tons of the precious metal. The lust for yet more gold drove the Spanish on, giving rise to the myth of El Dorado ('The Golden One'), a lost city ruled by a chieftain who covered himself in gold dust and bathed in a lake of gold.

But all this gold – real or imagined – paled into insignificance beside the major source of mineral wealth found in the Americas by the Spaniards: the silver-ore deposits at Potosí in the High Andes. Discovered in 1545, a settlement was established the following year and over more than two centuries of colonial control, some 45,000 tons of pure silver was extracted by slave labour from the Cerro Rico ('rich mountain') workings above the town. By the late 16th century, Potosí had made Spain far and away the wealthiest country in Europe. A mint was set up to strike coins on site in 1672. Dutch and English privateers tried to seize the bullion as it was shipped across the Atlantic, and German banking dynasties grew rich lending against repayment in silver.

Small wonder, then, that this financial engine-room of Spain's overseas empire became a byword for riches beyond the dreams of avarice. A variant of the idiom is *Valer un Perú* (though now in Bolivia, in colonial times Potosí fell within the Viceroyalty of Peru). The Spanish equivalent of Cockaigne/ *Schlaraffenland* (see p.233) also derives from this same area, with the wealthy mining settlement of Jauja in the Junín region becoming a proverbial land of plenty. *'Esto es Jauja!'* translates as 'This is the life!'

The British are altogether less euphoric about the source of their coinage: in an inversion of Polo's famous advertising slogan, locals refer to the South Wales town of Llantrisant as 'the hole with the Mint'.

CROSS THE RIVER WUPPER (GERMAN)

Über die Wupper gehen – **to vanish/to go West or go bust/ to die**

Ever since Virgil's 'grim ferryman' Charon rowed the souls of the dead across the Styx to the Underworld, crossing rivers has been a literary trope signifying a transition from one state to another. Perhaps the most famous was made by the Israelites when they crossed the River Jordan to land safe on Canaan's side.

Indeed, the final meaning of this idiom may well arise from a simple identification of 'crossing the Wupper' with 'crossing the Jordan', in its figurative sense of 'passing on to a better life', where the Land of Milk and Honey was equated to an afterlife in Heaven. But why especially the Wupper, hardly the largest or most famous of German rivers?

Rising in the Bergisch Land region of North Rhine–Westphalia, the Wupper runs for about 120 km south of Germany's industrial Ruhr region and flows into the Rhine at Leverkusen, just downstream of Cologne. The largest city on its course, Wuppertal, has a courthouse that was erected in 1834 on a small island in the river. Thirty years after its construction, a gaol with execution facilities (a guillotine) was built opposite, on the northern bank. Prisoners condemned to death in the court had to be taken across this arm of the Wupper for the sentence to be carried out. Bankrupts had their cases heard at an adjoining court on the island, so this geographical explanation also neatly accounts for the idiomatic sense of 'to go bust'.

Where vanishing is concerned, another historical factor comes into play. In the patchwork of petty principalities that preceded German unification in 1871, a stretch of the river east of Wuppertal formed the border between the County of Mark and the Duchy of Berg. While the former had long been subservient to Prussia's influence, the latter was placed under Prussian jurisdiction only at the Congress of Vienna in 1814. So, beginning with the reign of the 'Soldier King' Friedrich Wilhelm I (1713–40), the young men of the Mark were subject to Prussia's military draft, a brutal regime of harsh discipline and regular beatings (see **The Prussians don't shoot that fast**). Many chose to flee across the Wupper to the Duchy, where they were beyond the reach of the king's recruiting sergeants.

BE IN BABIA (Spanish)

Estar en Babia – **to have one's head in the clouds/to be distracted**

Babia is a mountainous region in the far north of León in northwest Spain. Now a province, from the 10th to the 13th centuries León was an independent state. It was also a far larger entity, which occupied the whole northwestern corner of the Iberian Peninsula, and its rulers played a major role in Spanish politics of the Middle Ages. Every summer, in order to escape the fearsome heat of the plains, the rulers of León would move north to Babia – in much the same way as administrators of the British Raj in India used to decamp to Simla in the Himalayan foothills.

Months would pass while the kings of León enjoyed the cool air of the Cordillera Cantábrica and the pleasures of the royal hunting lodge. While they were in retreat there, all business was suspended at court back in the capital city of León. Anyone seeking an audience with the monarch was simply informed 'Está in Babia'.

Over time, the phrase came to denote a state of being disengaged from the cares of the world, of figuratively being 'miles away'.

A FOOL'S PARADISE

A corpulent farmer lies flat on his back, waiting for food to drop into his mouth. Behind him, a mountain of buckwheat towers into the sky. Not, as it happens, a Eurosceptic view of the Common Agricultural Policy, but a scene from a much earlier period in the continent's history. 1567, to be exact, in Pieter Bruegel the Elder's painting *Het Luilekkerland*, which in English goes by the title *The Land of Cockaigne*. This richly symbolic picture – of which more presently – is just one manifestation of a concept that has been around for centuries: an imaginary land of plenty where everyone wallows in luxury and idleness.

The seductive idea of a world free of the tiresome necessity of work appears in the satire *The Amphictyons* by the 5th-century BC Greek poet Telecleides, who evokes a fictitious Golden Age of effortless plenty. In the 2nd century AD, the Greek writer Lucian also described a mock paradise of gross excess. By the time it assumes the name of Cocagne/Cokaygne, respectively in Middle French and Middle English poems of the 13th century, its allure has only increased – a fantastic parallel world to the nasty, brutish and short reality of medieval peasant life. In a modern translation, the Middle English poem begins:

> *Far in the sea to the west of Spain*
> *There is a land that we call Cokaygne;*
> *Under God's heaven no other land*
> *Such wealth and goodness has in hand*
> *Though paradise be merry and bright,*
> *Cokaygne is yet a fairer sight.*
> *For what is there in paradise*
> *But grass and flowers and green rice?*

Yet the rub comes in the etymology of the name of this otherworld. Deriving from the Middle Low German *kokenje* (a small, sweet cake distributed to children at seasonal fairs), it alludes to the materials from which the houses in the topsy-turvy land are said to be built. In other words, it's a form of paradise, but one so manifestly unreal

that you'd be an idiot to believe in it. The link is
made explicit in the cognate figurative terms *cucaña* in
Spanish and *cuccagna* in Italian, which both mean
'fool.'

Not that lands of plenty are an intrinsically foolish
proposition, at least not if you are an adherent of a
monotheistic faith. The Land of Milk and Honey is
promised to the Jews by Jehovah in Exodus 3:8 as a reward
for their exclusive devotion to Him. Tough luck if you
didn't happen to be born one of the Chosen People, so
medieval Christian theology shortened the odds by
holding out the prospect that anyone who performed good
works might gain their reward in heaven. But the point is
that these are *earned* states of paradise, part of a *quid pro
quo* between God and man.

By contrast, Bruegel's iconography makes it clear that
his *Luilekkerland* (a compound word meaning 'lazy,
luscious land') is an unearned life of ease. All elements of
the painting point to indulgence and gluttony. Tarts line
up neatly on a farmhouse roof, ready to be guzzled. In
the middle distance, a pig saunters by, its rump handily
speared with a carving knife, while between the dozing
farmer and a similarly prone clerk, a Hieronymus
Bosch-like hardboiled egg with legs scurries about, also
equipped with its own utensil. Lest we be in any doubt
about the polemical thrust of the piece, an engraving of
the painting attributed to Pieter van der Heyden in
around 1570 includes four lines of Flemish rhyme, which
in translation run:

All you loafers and gluttons always lying about,
Farmer, soldier, and clerk, you lie without work.
Here the fences are sausages, the houses are cake
And the fowl fly roasted, ready to eat.

This is not, though, just some unfocused diatribe against lazy individuals who expect something for nothing. The historical context in which Bruegel painted his picture reveals the true target of this and other contemporary counterblasts against excess. In 1494, the German scholar Sebastian Brant wrote the satire *Das Narrenschiff* ('The Ship of Fools') in which he laid bare the follies of the age. Narragonia, the fools' destination, closely resembles Cockaigne. Just over 30 years later, the Nuremberg poet and master-singer Hans Sachs (1494–1576) gave this same world a name that modern German still uses to signify a fools' paradise: *Schlaraffenland*. The root of this word was a Middle High German pejorative term (*sluraffe*) for a layabout. The humanist Brant, and the leading reformer Sachs, had a precise target in mind when they lambasted the indolent lifestyle: the Catholic Church and the secular authorities across Europe that were colluding with Rome to fleece ordinary people. Specifically, critics of Rome abhorred the Church's peddling of indulgences, promissory notes that supposedly entitled the bearer to remission of his or her sins and smoothed the path to Heaven. Literary works and pamphlets of the time abound in more or less veiled attacks on the voluptuaries of the Vatican.

By the time Bruegel completed his picture, the Reformation was well underway, the Peasants' War had ravaged Germany and been brutally suppressed, and the Low Countries were in open revolt against their Catholic Spanish overlords. A reformer's distaste shines through his portrayal of the three representative figures of the parasitical class: their dissolute behaviour is the antithesis of what German sociologist Max Weber would later call the 'Protestant work ethic'.

Index